Privacy in America

DAVID F. LINOWES

Privacy
in America

Is Your Private Life in the Public Eye?

University of Illinois Press
Urbana and Chicago

© 1989 by the Board of Trustees of the University of Illinois
Manufactured in the United States of America
C 5 4 3 2 1

This book is printed on acid-free paper.

Library of Congress Cataloging-in-Publication Data

Linowes, David F.
    Privacy in America / David F. Linowes.
        p.   cm.
    Includes index.
    ISBN 0-252-01604-1 (alk. paper)
    1. Privacy, Right of—United States.   2. Computers—United States—
Access control.   3. Records—United States—Access control.
I. Title.
JC596.2.U5L56   1989
323.44′83—dc19   88-20645
                                                              CIP

Dedicated to my grandchildren
Shelby, Robert, and Jennifer, and
their generation who will inherit
only those freedoms we preserve today.

Contents

Preface

This book is for the millions of Americans who go to work each day, buy with credit cards, visit doctors, enter their children in schools, join clubs, write checks, or take out insurance. To participate in these activities requires that we give up bits of personal information about ourselves. This data is entered in data banks, but does not necessarily remain there.

Unknown to the average person, there has developed an immense underground of collected personal, often sensitive, information about each man, woman, and child in America. Do you know all the people who get this material, and what they do with it? Does it affect your life for good or evil? It's a message that needs to be told, and I am telling it here.

Computer technology that so dramatically adds to our personal conveniences carries with it a vulnerability to abuses. Being fully aware of this vulnerability not only helps us protect ourselves against personal abuses, but strengthens our democracy by building a bulwark of an informed populace.

Personal information in the hands of governmental authorities, employers, insurance companies, financial institutions, and credit-reporting companies can be and is being used in ways you never intend when you disclose sensitive information. Furthermore, decisions are routinely made on the basis of information that may be incorrect, outdated, or simply irrelevant.

Silently but relentlessly the computer is making it easy for big business and government to erode our "right to be let alone." More people know more things about you than ever before. This book tells you who those people are, what they are doing with that information, and how you can defend yourself. It tells about privacy in America.

Information privacy means different things to different people. In venturing to define it, I am tempted to borrow the observation made by Supreme Court

Justice Potter Stewart, who when confronted with a case involving obscenity said he could not define obscenity, "but I know it when I see it." I think we all know the abuse of information privacy when we see it.

In this book I am recommending fair information practices in dealings between an individual and an institution. Such practices should minimize intrusiveness, e.g., a banker should not demand and you should not disclose more personal information than necessary to process a loan application. These practices also should ensure fairness, e.g., an employer should tell an employee what kind of data is being accumulated in a personnel file, and why. Finally, they should provide for legally enforcible expectations of confidentiality, e.g., you expect confidentiality when you tell your physician personal information about your intimate relationships. The physician as well as the medical secretary, file clerk, receptionist, accountant, insurance carrier, and others should be required by law (which should include penalty provisions) to keep that data confidential.

These principles of fair information practice and how they are being violated are the subject of the ensuing chapters, along with safeguards for you to apply.

Acknowledgments

My appreciation goes to Lawrence J. Malley, Associate Director of the University of Illinois Press, who instigated the preparation of the manuscript, prodded its completion, and expedited it through the many stages of the publication process.

I thank the Institute of Government and Public Affairs and its director, Robert F. Rich, as well as the Research Board of the University of Illinois who underwrote the 1987 survey reported in Chapter 4, "How Your Employer Is Handling Your Personal Information: A Survey of Individual Privacy Protection in Big Business." It was Diane M. O'Rourke, Project Coordinator, who personally supervised the final, high professional quality of that assignment. The recommendations in that chapter essentially are based on those designed by the United States Privacy Protection Commission (USPPC), which I chaired, and were contained in the report I presented to the President and the Congress in July 1977. They are as relevant today as they were then.

I am grateful to my administrative secretary, Jean C. Poole, who painstakingly guided the manuscript through its several drafts, at times participating in the research effort as well. Ray C. Spencer, my research assistant, helped with the research and documentation, always with pleasant enthusiasm. Mark R. Filip competently assisted with that work.

David F. Linowes

1

Introduction

If I were asked what the greatest danger is today in the conduct of democracy's affairs I suppose I would think first of war—but second, and immediately—we in America are becoming so big, so organized, so institutionalized that there is increasing danger that the individual and his precious diversity will be squeezed out completely.

—*Adlai Ewing Stevenson*

The explosion in computer and telecommunication technology is having revolutionary impacts on every aspect of our personal and institutional lives. Gross world consumption of information technology exceeds $1 trillion annually, and in the 1990s this figure is expected to reach $2 trillion, with North Americans producing and consuming half this amount. Do all the changes being brought about by these marvels of technology enhance our well-being now and for the future, or should we be alert to elements of danger? In writing about the new electronic technology for the National Academy of Sciences, in an essay published in *Technological Frontiers and Foreign Relations* (1985), Simon Ramo warned, "Today it is clear that the impact has become so deep and pervasive and the changes are coming so rapidly that all of our organized ways of approaching national and international social, political, and economic adjustments are suddenly out-of-date. Our ability to respond is in jeopardy. It is incumbent upon us to recognize this as we try to understand what the technology impact is all about."

As so often happened in history, with each new technological breakthrough we become so carried away with the exciting new advances and expectations that we tend to ignore the sometimes harmful consequences that may ensue until damage has occurred. The electronic revolution now taking place is changing our way of life more profoundly than did the Industrial Revolution over a century ago. Are you prepared to deal with the threats to your well-being as well as the benefits it is bringing?

Now that electronic technology is relentlessly engulfing our daily activities, we should pause to examine the potential problems that silently lurk behind the computer terminal. Years ago, Congress sought to deal with some of the dangers that could occur from the limitless accumulations of personal data in computers by enacting the Privacy Act of 1974. That act placed some constraints on federal records and established the U.S. Privacy Protection Commission to examine all actual and potential abuses of personal privacy in the private and public sectors.

My intensive involvement with the substance of this book began when I chaired that commission. In a way, the Privacy Act was a reflexive response to the shocking revelations of the Watergate episode. For the first time, Congress responded to the decade of aggressive proddings by Senator Sam Ervin who had been sounding the alarm of the dangers to our way of life being created by the massive accumulations of individually identifiable sensitive data.

On 17 July 1977, I presented the report of the commission to President Carter at a special ceremony held for that occasion in the Cabinet Room of the White House and to a joint meeting of committees of the Senate and House held on the afternoon of the same day. Since that time, I have had many opportunities to evaluate the concerns sounded in our report and to relate them to everyday actions by government officials and corporate executives. My observation posts have included chairmanships of other Presidential and Congressional commissions and memberships on boards of directors of several leading corporations. What follows are some of the disturbing perceptions of the lengthening shadows over the free and casual lifestyle we in the United States have been privileged to enjoy for two centuries.

First, some comments are in order about the miraculous breakthroughs being created by ever-advancing computer technology, which gives man extensions of the human mind and memory beyond the dreams of the most visionary science fiction writers. As Charles Van Doren put it in "Why the Computer Is Only as Good as It Is" (in *Great Ideas Today*, 1985), the computer "does not extend the mind merely; it extends the power, skill, and competence of the whole human being." Technology we currently have in place is at least a hundred years behind what has already been developed. Scientists project entire libraries on a silicon chip, all factory controls on a silicon wafer.

It is a fact that we learned more about the human brain in the decade of the 1970s than we had in the rest of history. That knowledge of the brain is being recreated in the computers of the 1980s and 1990s.

Artificial Intelligence

Considerable progress has been made in programming computers to think like human beings by using ultrasophisticated software. This software—commonly known as "artificial intelligence" (AI)—will be in widespread commercial use within the next decade. Artificial intelligence enables computers to draw useful inferences from outside data so that limited spheres of human activity can be understood and predicted. Artificial intelligence combined with visual processing and voice recognition has already made an impact in the development of test equipment in the laboratory. For instance, a medical testing machine "sees" red blood cells and decides whether or not they are healthy. Systems have been developed which recognize up to ten thousand spoken words. For the future, experts predict that the computer will be as easy to use as the telephone, will understand continuous spoken speech, and will be able to translate any language.

One of the fathers of artificial intelligence, Herbert Simon of Carnegie-Mellon University, maintains that computers can be programmed to learn in nearly the same ways that humans do. "You give the computer a problem and it can't do it. Then you give it certain experiences, in this case some worked-out examples, and after it has examined the examples then it can do problems like the one it originally failed on," Simon told *Science Magazine* and *Psychology Today* staff writer Constance Holden in 1986. Simon does not see any limits to the capacity of computers to model human thought processes. In the future, according to Simon, it may be possible to "store away the equivalent of a representative human being" within a computer.

AI is being used to solve complex mathematical problems and to make medical diagnoses. Computers at NASA are performing over six billion arithmetical calculations a second. The human mind is no match for this speed. Researchers at IBM, Texas Instruments, and Genentech are applying artificial intelligence to analyze geological formations, to design new biological genes, and to read, digest, and answer correspondence.

At the turn of the century, French author Paul Valéry, observing the bursting seeds of the Industrial Revolution, wrote, "The trouble with our times is that the future is not what it used to be." Today, this is more so. The computer is recasting our lives in more profound ways than did the printing press five hundred years ago. Obviously, we cannot sit idly by. It was Sir Francis Bacon who warned, "He who will not apply new remedies must expect new evils."

The ways that we think and even what we think is often governed by the tools we have to express those thoughts. With electronic technology, a whole new spectrum of expression and thought now beckons the human mind. J. David Balter in his *Turing's Man—Western Culture in the Computer Age* (1984) puts it, "For over 2,000 years the tools of thought changed little in essence—basically they were ink, paper, and some means of applying one to the other. But the computer will surely give intellectual activity a new shape."

Personal computers are already giving advice and assistance in many human activities. Programs are being designed to adapt to individual styles. Such machines are not dreams, they are here. At Tsukuba Expo '85 held in Japan, Hitachi featured a robot who vacuumed, cooked dinner, and did what most housekeepers refuse to do—it washed windows. Matsushita's robot used advanced sensor technology to sketch lifelike portraits. It is estimated that there are currently between sixteen thousand and seventeen thousand robots in use in the United States alone. Over twelve hundred laboratory robots are mixing and measuring chemicals and medications. In the future, these service robots will be used on oil rigs, in hospitals, gas stations, and fast-food outlets. They may also have a future fighting fires and testing high-tension electric lines. Today, these machines are widely used in nuclear power plants and in undersea work where it might be dangerous or costly to place human workers.

Some applications are creating "expert" systems. That is, computers are programmed to duplicate the decision-making process of a leading expert in a given field. These programs are designed by first keying all known information on a given subject into the computer. Then, programmers interview a recognized expert at great length to determine precisely how he or she processes information to form judgments. That knowledge is then codified so computers can make similar decisions by emulating the human process of inferential reasoning.

In Britain a computerized detective called Holmes—the Home Office Large Major Enquiry System—is used to aid police investigations by storing and analyzing large amounts of data gathered from thousands of day-to-day police reports. In just seconds, the system can make rapid connections between seemingly unrelated events and speed the investigation of cases such as so-called serial crimes. Current plans call for the computerized linking of all seventy-five divisions of the London Metropolitan Police using about two thousand microcomputers linked to eight mainframe computers. The new system, called Crime Report Information System (CRIS), will supplement Holmes and should be operational by 1991.

"Thinking" computers will replace people in millions of jobs in many industries and offices. Currently, twenty-eight million people are employed in manufacturing in America. Intelligent computers could take over twenty-five million of those jobs.

Although still in its infancy, this "knowledge engineering" has already been used with some success in prospecting for minerals, diagnosing diseases, analyzing chemicals, selecting antibiotics, and configuring computers. Other applications of expert systems include such diverse tasks as evaluating casualty insurance risks, making commercial-credit decisions, and controlling oil-well drilling.

Stanford researchers have developed a program called Eurisko that enables a computer to develop its own theories and ideas once it is given the principles of a discipline. At Yale, scientists have trained a computer to interpret newspaper articles that it reads with an optical scanning device. The school has one program that correlates stories about terrorism, and the computer is becoming an expert at knowing what terrorists want and need. Eventually, researchers expect that computers will become voracious readers, constantly updating their reservoirs of knowledge. General-purpose scanning machines are currently being produced in quantity. Technological advances and rapidly declining prices make these print-to-digital converters adaptable to a large number of specialized applications.

Control Data Corporation has developed a "medically smart" computer called HELP (Health Evaluation through Logical Processing) that is bringing a technological revolution to medicine. A study of LDS Hospital in Salt Lake City revealed that doctors who used the HELP program changed their prescriptions for their patients 80 percent of the time after receiving a drug alert from the computer.

Police departments are using computerized fingerprint identification systems to catch criminals. Approximately seventy-five jurisdictions in eighteen states are using automated fingerprint checking in which prints from a data base of hundreds of thousands of files are compared with those obtained from a crime scene. Within just a few seconds, the computer finds the ten closest print matches and final identification is then made by fingerprint experts.

A new device called Veridex uses optical scanning and a laser printer to produce digitized topographical fingerprints without ink. Prints are made by simply running the scanner over the finger and can be electronically transmitted to automated fingerprint files. Britain's Aberdeen University has developed a computerized face-recognition system. Information from witnesses is used to put together a suspect profile. The computer then chooses pictures of possible candidates from its files based on forty-nine different facial characteristics.

A number of companies, such as Texas Instruments, are already marketing devices capable of synthesizing words. Within a few years, computers will be able to understand complete sentences so that typewriters can take dictation. IBM has a machine called EPISTLE (Executive-Principle's Intelligent System for Text and Linguistic Endeavors) capable of reading business mail, understanding and summarizing the contents, and replying on its own. Hewlett-Packard is developing an "intelligent" electronic mail system that not only forwards messages, but also generates its own responses.

In the 1990s people will be able to talk to computers with the ease with which we talk to one another. Some computers already allow communication in written English. To give computers fluency, AI researchers at the University of Illinois, Yale, and IBM are programming machines with two types of knowledge. First, they instruct the computer on rules of grammar and syntax. Then they give the computer knowledge about the world.

Japanese and Western commitments for the "fifth generation" of computing will commercially produce intelligent machines that interact with people naturally. The machines being developed will respond to our questions and instructions in our own language. Computers are being programmed to translate from one language to another. Fujitsu has such a translation system.

A speech-synthesis device which reads out loud information stored in its data bank is being placed on the market by Digital Equipment Corporation. It will have an unlimited vocabulary and can be stocked with unlimited data. This innovation will be a boon for the blind or for the slow or lazy reader.

It can be argued that in the age of interactive telecommunications, physical distance has little meaning. People do not need to remain crowded in or near employment centers or marketing areas. They interact with others from wherever they are. Centralized buildings and congested cities of the industrial age are becoming increasingly unnecessary. They are giving way to teleconferencing, electronic funds, teleshopping, teleducation, telemedicine, and even telegambling. In Hong Kong, three hundred thousand telebettors make their wagers electronically.

In education, private enterprise has already introduced what it called the world's first electronic university. Through the "Telelearning" system, instructors for 150 courses, including courses in art, finance, and business administration, can be taught through one-on-one courses using personal computers over telephone lines. There is no technical barrier to the fulfillment of a complete educational experience from a computer in one's own home. Some authorities talk of eliminating the social addiction of attending school.

In some private schools students use the computer as others use books and blackboards. In those schools, children have electronic pen pals in various countries around the globe. Via satellite, each youngster communicates in his own language and thereby learns the other person's language.

Adverse Impacts on Personal Lives

Meanwhile, some of the applications of computers are creating disturbing signs of overbearing "Big Brother."

Surveillance of workers on assembly lines, in offices, and in stores is now more intense than ever before. With computerized electronic devices, office and factory productivity is constantly monitored. In the much-advertised electronic office, data-processing machines are both work tools and monitoring devices. Productivity and employee behavior, including that of executives, are watched.

Computer monitoring is being used in some businesses to keep track of employees second-by-second as they work. It monitors such things as the number of key strokes per hour for typists, or the amount of time telephone operators spend on the phone with each caller. Administrators claim the purpose of the monitoring is to improve supervision over employees and to help determine who is eligible for promotion or salary increases.

Seven million workers nationwide are linked to computers through video display terminals, and one-third of them are believed to be monitored by computer. Critics of the system say it is counterproductive because it can lead to increased stress, fatigue, and turnover among workers. They also say workers are sometimes unfairly judged for falling below predetermined, arbitrary goals set with the aid of computer monitoring. For example, it was reported in the press that Maevon Garrett of Baltimore, Maryland, who had spent eighteen years with AT&T, felt he was unfairly fired in 1984 from his job when the computer revealed he took an average of thirty seconds per caller.

Increasingly in places of employment workers inform the computer when they go to the restroom. Through magnetized ID cards, employees are automatically checked in and out as they go from one location to another.

While they are not allowed in advertising, subliminal messages are now being used increasingly in the workplace. Audio subliminals are being played over public-address systems in stores to deter shoplifting and in dentists' offices to relieve patient anxiety. Some businesses use them to boost employee morale and productivity. Often, firms want to keep their use of subliminals secret to lessen the chance of employee opposition. Currently, no federal laws ban such messages, although the Federal Communications Commission code suggests their use is not in the public interest. In an attempt to counter the potential abuses posed by new subliminal products which claim to modify employee attitudes, the California legislature recently approved a bill which prohibits audio and visual subliminals in the workplace.

Common usage of computers in business, government, education, and personal life brings with it the need to redefine and reapply common ethical practices and personal behavior. Unauthorized intrusions into electronic data banks have become looked upon as challenging games by young people at all levels. Hacking, now by common usage defined as the systematic probing for entry codes into other people's data banks, is rapidly becoming the universal pastime for young people with technological or scientific skills. These unauthorized intrusions go on every day. Only a fraction receive press attention.

For example, in Milwaukee, Wisconsin, teenagers gained access to the computer system in the Sloan-Kettering Cancer Center in New York, changing files concerning radiation treatment. In another case, a computer hobbyist tried to shut down the Columbia University computer and caused thousands of dollars in damage and the loss of a great amount of data. Neither Sloan-Kettering nor Columbia took legal criminal action because lawyers could not agree that any laws in effect at the time were broken. In another case, federal investigators charged that students at the University of Southern California had infiltrated the computer system, changing grades and creating fraudulent Ph.D. degrees, which they sold for as much as $25,000 each. Our ethical behavior concerning respect for other people's records kept in a file cabinet has not yet been extended to the same records when they are transposed into electronic form.

A disturbing incident of computer infiltration occurred in November 1988. A renegade virus, a small software program developed apparently by a graduate student at Cornell University, used loopholes in communication networks to invade multiple research sites such as NASA's Ames Research Center, Los Alamos National Laboratory, Argonne National Laboratory, and a number of research facilities in universities nationwide. Once inside a system, the program used distribution lists stored there to rapidly infect other locations. While it is believed this incident caused little or no permanent damage, the virus did make numerous attacks, 2,000 at the University of Maryland alone. This shows how vulnerable computer systems could be to mass abuse. Experts fear that similar viruses could destroy valuable data and disrupt national security or defense computers.

These are not uniquely American concerns, but are shared worldwide. Multinational conferences have been held to debate implications of data compilation and transfer. In 1983, following an enormous public protest, the Constitutional Court of the Federal Republic of Germany cancelled the normal decennial population census on the grounds that the government had failed to protect individuals' rights to privacy. In Japan, 61 percent of the respondents to a 1985 poll conducted by the prime minister's office said they were interested in protecting privacy, compared with 25 percent in a similar poll taken nine years ago. Numerous countries have adopted privacy legislation mandating fair information practices.

Everyone Is Affected by Data in Computers

Along with the intelligence now being stored in computer memories throughout the world, there is detailed personal, sensitive information about all of us in existing data banks of government agencies, corporations, educational institutions, and religious organizations.

What happens to this computerized data? Is it accurate? Who has access to it? How is it used to make decisions about what job or promotion you get, whether your bank loan request or insurance application is approved, what school your children get into, and whether you get that credit card? Do you know who is maintaining an ongoing record about your activities, and why?

The ensuing chapters will deal with these and many other concerns, as well as suggest what you can do about them. The discussion will reveal the impacts computerized personal information is having increasingly on many aspects of your way of life. Problems exist when ideas are absent. The problems that exist can be corrected, but it will take personal initiative by each of us.

Conclusion

Although computers offer great hope and promise for the future, they also have potential for harm. One must constantly be alert to the new dangers created by the rapid advances in technology. Computers have many beneficial applications, but they also have produced infringements on the individual's right to privacy. Vast amounts of personal information are being amassed without the subject's knowledge, and preserved indefinitely to be retrieved instantly. This information can be used in ways that have disturbing implications for an individual's personal freedom.

The legal system has lagged far behind new technological advances. As a result, society is inadequately protected from some white-collar crimes, as well as from unethical practices. Laws which were adequate in the relatively recent past must be redefined to cover new applications of computer technology. In order to protect his personal privacy an individual must first be informed.

Armed with knowledge of potential dangers, we can contribute to shaping a public policy that secures the advantages of computer technology while minimizing the threats to personal freedom.

2

The Issues

The forces allied against the individual have never been greater.

—*William O. Douglas*

Recently a copy of a computer password directory was stolen from a national computer company that leased time to America's largest corporations. With this directory, a criminal or vandal could enter any individual customer's file or personal account and change, delete, or extract anything in it. No one would be able to detect the theft or manipulation. No one would know if a payment record or personal credit file had been changed or if that information had been extracted.

Donn Parker, a senior management systems consultant at SRI International, says in his book *Computer Security Management* that, fundamentally, we do not know how to protect large-scale, multi-access computer systems. He asserts, "EDP [electronic data processing] audit techniques and adaptations or traditional security practices can do no more than contain the problem today. They can't protect society from computer abuse perpetrated by the computer systems programmers, computer operators, and maintenance engineers. No practical way has been devised to audit the work of these people sufficiently because of the increasing complexity of computer systems and the lack of standards, discipline, and structured practices in their design and construction."

Personal Files and What They Mean to You

Whether you like it or not, your personal information is probably not confidential. More likely, it is the subject of countless files that are available to people who are total strangers to you. Mammoth data banks maintained by private companies are, for a price, open to others; one consumer reporting company, for example, prepares up to thirty-five million individual credit reports annually. Silently, but relentlessly, the computer is eroding your "right to be let alone." More people know more about you than ever before. Do you know who has that sensitive information and what they do with it?

Records, regardless of their accuracy, could cost you a job or a promotion. They could result in the denial of credit or a life insurance policy. Or they could taint your reputation. Chances are if you do have the luck or perseverance to unearth these files, or to discover mistakes, you will very likely be helpless to do anything about them. Errors, once recorded, become accepted as truths.

To be sure, much of this information is legitimately obtained and properly used. The massive, highly automated data-collection networks that pervade the country are rarely used for malicious purposes. But the fact remains that most Americans have no idea of the scope of these record-keeping practices, and they would be shocked to learn how easy it is to obtain information they had assumed to be confidential. Applying for life insurance, buying a TV on credit, opening a bank account, or filling out various forms in order to get hospitalization or insurance benefits are just a few of the activities which serve to inject personal information into the network. And this information has value. Not only is it used as a tool for those who make business and government decisions, but it is marketable for a variety of commercial purposes and, increasingly, as an instrument of surveillance.

When record-keeping technology was primitive, the problems of abuse were relatively minor. But as this technology grows ever more sophisticated, these problems take on major significance.

Few, if any, countries collect more information on their citizens than Sweden, where each resident is assigned a ten-digit "person number." These identification numbers make access to personal data easy and facilitate data-bank linking. It is not uncommon for the average Swede to be listed in at least one hundred official registers. Swedish citizens are becoming increasingly concerned about the accessibility of these files. Recently it was disclosed that nearly fifteen thousand people had been secretly studied for twenty years by a team of Swedish sociologists through the use of computerized official records. All ten-year-olds who lived in Stockholm in 1963 were selected for the study without their informed consent. Information collected on the subjects included marital status, family size, income, school grades, test scores, and employment records. Sweden places a high priority on social research, and much of the data collected in the project was purchased from the government. Records of income, taxes paid, and property holdings, and even passport or driver's license photographs are available to anyone—the photographs cost about forty cents each. Another Swedish study investigating a possible link between abortions and cancer used records of 165,000 women without their consent. Sweden's Data Inspection Board, which licenses individuals, organizations, and businesses keeping computerized personal files on citizens, has ordered that computer tapes identifying the subjects in both studies be destroyed.

Although storing and retrieving millions of pieces of information is not dangerous in itself, information can be abused or taken out of context, and that can sometimes cause serious hardships for people. For example, journalist and author David Burnham reported in *The Rise of the Computer State* (1983) how a company formed by Harvey Saltz, a former deputy district attorney in Los Angeles, caused a few problems for renters. Saltz set up a company called U.D. Registry, Inc., which used a computer to store information about legal charges filed by landlords in the courts. Saltz's purpose in starting the company was to provide information to landlords about unreliable tenants. The tenants, however, knew nothing about the listing.

One tenant, Lucky Kellener, was listed in the computer files as being an unreliable renter. When he went searching for a larger apartment, he was turned away. After the third rejection he learned that he was listed as "undesirable." The listing came about because a few years earlier he paid the rent for his brother, who was later evicted. Kellener was included in the court papers, and this information was used to declare him unreliable. Another victim of the computer was Barbara Ward, who rented an apartment in Los Angeles. She soon discovered that the apartment was infested with rodents and roaches. She decided to give the landlord thirty days' notice after he refused to deal with the situation. The landlord, however, had issued an eviction notice before she left. The case eventually was thrown out of court. Since the registry listed her as being served with an eviction notice, she had difficulty renting an apartment several months later.

Apart from the chance that innocent errors produced by extensive information-sharing will be spread and multiplied, there is the danger that irrelevant data will end up in the wrong place and still have an impact. Information in a psychiatric record, for example, may have an entirely new and mistaken significance when it crops up in an employer's or credit bureau's file. And we have no choice but to submit to the established current modes of institutionalized practice. To go without insurance, hospitalization, banking, credit, or formal education is nearly unthinkable.

At the same time, managers are justified in striving to minimize the risks in their decision making. The more information they have, and the more accurate, the greater their chances of success. But there is the risk that government and private organizations will have too much access to personal information, and too much control over individual citizens. Freedom is like a bucket of water. If there is a small personal-information leak, in time all freedom runs out. The abuse of power based on accumulated pieces of information is not a myth.

An Uncertain Legal Matter

No less a figure than Supreme Court Justice Louis Brandeis spoke in 1890 of the individual's right to be let alone as being the most valued right of civilized people. And as far back as 1868, Michigan State Supreme Court Judge Cooley ruled privacy to be the constitutional right to be let alone. In fact, privacy rights are not specifically identified in the Constitution, but the implication is clearly there. The Third Amendment prohibits the lodging of soldiers in private homes without the owner's consent. The Fourth Amendment protects citizens against arbitrary government search. Supreme Court Justice Potter Stewart singled out this amendment to observe, "The Fourth Amendment and the personal rights it secures have a long history. At the very core stands the right of a man to retreat into his own home and there be free from unreasonable governmental intrusion." And courts have been interpreting a right to privacy from the Fifth Amendment that protects against self-incrimination, the First Amendment that provides for freedom of speech and assembly, and the Ninth Amendment that reserves to the people all rights not specifically delegated to the states and the federal government.

It was the Privacy Act of 1974 that for the first time gave statutory recognition to a right of privacy. It set up certain constraints on federal agencies. Unfortunately, while the law in general implies rights to privacy, there is inadequate specific protection and too much ambiguity in it.

Those limited rights that the individual does have in his relations to the federal government often require that he take the initiative. There is an endless list of records kept about an individual of which he is not likely to be aware. How then can he spot errors in his records? Even if he did spot errors, it would be most difficult to find their origin since the sources of the information concerning him would not usually be clearly noted. It is also impossible for him to know whether organizations with which he assumes he has a confidential relationship honor that expectation of confidentiality. When he does know that a record is being abused or suspects an error in it, he rarely knows how to exercise whatever limited rights he has.

There have been few court cases dealing with personal-information privacy, and therefore we have few judicial precedents. In the past, bureaucratic and physical limitations had been unwitting protectors of privacy. The bulk of personal records accumulated by government agencies, corporations, or institutions stayed within those organizations. There was no mass transfer of information. Retrieving one record out of a million was awkward and could take months. Also, because storage of accumulated data was costly, much of it was destroyed within a reasonable time after use. This is no longer true.

Today, the transfer of vast amounts of selected information is accomplished at the speed of light. Storage units are so tiny that it may cost less to store data than to destroy it, since deleting files is a process which may consume valuable computer time. The result is that massive amounts of personal data are being accumulated in the nation's growing battery of data banks. And the individual is lost. He becomes a number among millions of numbers bunched into profile groupings. Mahatma Gandhi warned that no society can possibly be built on a denial of the individual when he observed, "If the individual ceases to count, what is left of society?"

Personal Privacy and Efficient Management

Some observers refer to the information privacy problem as one of "information pollution," and liken it to the handling of toxic waste. Scientists have not yet given us the practical means for safely disposing of either. Much data is being routinely transferred from data bank to data bank. If administrators are concerned at all for the protection of individual, sensitive data, it is at best of secondary importance to accomplishing the organization's goal. This is understandable in view of the job responsibilities of managers.

Often, firms require employees to submit to a urinalysis as a prerequisite to obtaining or keeping a job. Urinalysis testing by Fortune 500 companies increased from 20 percent in 1985 to 40 percent in 1987, according to CompuChem Laboratories, Inc., a national drug-testing firm. Drug testing has become a $300 million-a-year industry for businesses producing urinalysis kits and operating diagnostic labs. The practice of testing for drug use is spreading rapidly in an effort to lessen accidents, absenteeism, and low productivity. Employers are beginning to test workers already on the payroll, and some school systems are considering testing both teachers and students. Critics say tests are often inaccurate and that the drugs detected have no effect on job performance.

A 1986 survey of 497 national companies conducted by the College Placement Council found that nearly 30 percent of employers of new college graduates required drug screening, usually including urinalysis. Almost all of the firms having screening programs tested for both marijuana and hard drugs. Safety was listed as the primary reason for the testing of job applicants, and most firms using the screening reported that they would not hire applicants who failed drug tests. A survey of Fortune 500 companies conducted at the University of Illinois and reported in Chapter 4, below, found that 58 percent of the companies have a drug-testing program in operation. Nine out of ten of them conducted the test for pre-employment screenings.

Some people claim that urinalysis can show whether a person is being treated for a heart condition, epilepsy, diabetes, or asthma, and that such screening can become more of a device for monitoring off-the-job activity than a test for actual job performance. Most of the tests do not determine if drugs are actually used on the job or the extent to which drugs interfere with job performance. Often, cocaine can be detected in the urine up to three days after consumption. Trace chemicals may be present from five days to three weeks after marijuana is used. Over-the-counter drugs, such as Advil and Nuprin, have shown up as illegal drugs in some tests. False accusations of marijuana abuse may result from fragments of the skin pigment melanin that can be detected in the urine. Melanin, which is present in everyone but is usually at higher levels among blacks and Hispanics, can break down and produce positive results in urinalysis testing even for people who have never used marijuana.

The U.S. military spends about $100 for the collection, transportation, analysis, and reporting of each test in its urinalysis program. If each employee in the U.S. work force were to be tested in a similar manner, the cost to society would be $8 to $10 billion per year.

General Motors, the nation's largest private employer, decided to hire undercover agents from a private detective firm to work on assembly lines in their plants to combat drug and alcohol abuse problems. The company estimates that such abuses involve at least one out of every ten workers. While the sting operation led to the arrest of nearly two hundred people, most of whom were GM employees, union leaders complained that this tactic was unprofessional and unfairly concentrated on union members instead of management. Are undercover agents being hired by some companies to obtain other kinds of personal information about employees, without their knowledge?

A 1982 survey conducted by the Office of Technology Assessment, a bipartisan agency that serves Congress, found that eighteen major U.S. companies had used genetic screening of employees to test for high vulnerability to toxins. Genetic screening is used to identify individuals susceptible to disease caused by dust or fumes in the workplace. One genetic test probes for a gene called HDL (high density lipoprotein). HDL influences the body's ability to remove cholesterol from tissues. People with high HDL levels are less susceptible to heart attacks. Genetic monitoring involves periodic checks of employees to determine signs of chromosomal abnormalities such as those influencing cancer or miscarriage rates among women due to workplace chemicals or radiation exposure. While employers say the tests lower medical costs and enable susceptible workers to avoid hazardous employment, many labor leaders and those concerned with personal privacy see dangers in labeling certain individuals or groups as "high risk." Such labeling could involve a loss of career or health insurance coverage for the worker. Problems may also extend to a specific race being singled out and denied certain types of employment. Also, employers may face lawsuits for failing to dismiss susceptible employees. While current genetic tests cannot account for the effects of confounding factors such as smoking, drinking, or inherited illness, experts say that within two or three years the technology of the screening may advance to the point where such tests could be made mandatory for companies in high-risk industries.

Some managers argue that the forces of efficient management run counter to the forces of human privacy protection. However, nothing can be considered right from the standpoint of efficiency if it is wrong morally. Those who think there is a basic conflict between long-term management effectiveness and safeguarding personal privacy rights must either be inexperienced in the art and science of long-term management or ignorant of the consequences of personal-privacy abuses, including their own.

Computer Crime—The New Frontier

There is an alarming growth of computer crime which, apart from the obvious losses to individual businesses and the economy as a whole, constitutes a danger to privacy in all its aspects. As society grows increasingly dependent on the computer, a fertile field opens up to sophisticated criminals who have the technological know-how to tap, manipulate, and alter electronic information. Many computer programmers and other electronic data-processing employees—there are well over two million nationwide—have access to sensitive, computerized data and are technically capable of using that data without authorization. The nature of electronic technology is such that entry into a data bank is very difficult if not impossible to detect.

For example, a federal employee diverted $100,000 in an eighteen-month period by reactivating accounts of dead beneficiaries and creating fictitious accounts. A computer programmer used his agency's computer to run a football pool, calculating odds, printing football schedules, and keeping track of bets. An engineer, using his employer's computer, maintained records of his personal consulting business and sent data to his customers. All these abuses were discovered by accident, and the full extent of the financial losses could never be determined.

In Connecticut, a part-time policeman was suspected of obtaining information from the police computer for his full-time employer. He was not charged, however, because he had not violated state law.

The programming of photographs into computers to improve images is already being done, but the legal and ethical ramifications of computerized photographic image enhancement have yet to be explored. Through the manipulation of individual picture elements, people could be pictured in places they never were or dressed in clothes they had never worn. Although the enhancement procedure can be detected with the assistance of a computer by comparing the new photograph with the original, once the photograph has been printed and the original destroyed, there is no record of that original. Furthermore, a manipulated photograph can be rephotographed, and prints made from the resulting negative would not reveal any manipulation.

Telephone accessibility has increased the computer's vulnerability. Whiz-kid programmers see breaking a system's defenses as a game. And they keep trying until they succeed. Most experts agree that foolproof safeguards for computer files seem unlikely for some time to come. "You must realize," notes a former Central Intelligence Agency employee, "that there is no such thing as an entirely secure electronic-data or voice-communication network anywhere."

Many companies use computer time-sharing networks such as Telenet or Tymshare for easy access to their computer from anywhere that has a touch-tone phone. Users need only enter a password to get access. The reality of these systems is that passwords are often handed out freely, or are predictable enough to guess. If the passwords are not changed often, they are even easier prey to hobbyists and criminals.

Do You Know Where Your Personal Data Is?

Most people are not aware of the names of organizations that have access to intimate information about them. For example, most of us probably only associate California-based TRW, one of the largest technological companies in the world, with aerospace or sophisticated engineering. However, one of its subsidiaries is among the largest credit-reporting bureaus in the nation, having as many as 133 million personal dossiers in its system, most likely including yours and mine. These dossiers can be transmitted with the speed of light through the sky, across the nation, and abroad to its subscribers to be used for any purpose. Chapter 9, "Credit: The Record-Keeping Explosion," describes the workings of credit-reporting companies and the many problems resulting from errors and the misuse of personal data.

Telephones

As computers and related technology improve, so does the potential to keep track of citizens. In the telephone industry, new advances allow local telephone companies to itemize a customer's local calls just as they have been doing for years with long-distance calls. This increased record keeping has serious implications for intrusion. According to Washington, D.C., People's Counsel

Brian Lederer, "The implications are just staggering. Who you call gives somebody more information about your business, social, political, and religious affiliations than any other piece of information. All our constitutional liberties are lost once somebody else gets ahold of those records."

Those that disagree point to such facts as AT&T's voluntary guidelines that allow release of calling records only under subpoena or court order, except for national security investigations. But with so much turmoil in the telephone industry today, how long will those voluntary safeguards remain in effect? What about the many other companies now supplying telephone service?

Market Research

Traditionally, research on people's buying habits has been carried out with diaries which allow consumers to enter the purchases they make. Now, more reliable information sources are being used to help companies keep track of consumer tastes. Many companies, such as Campbell Soup, Procter and Gamble, and General Foods, are using high-tech market research to evaluate new products and to determine what marketing strategies will be most effective. New methods of electronic testing allow researchers to observe consumer behavior without letting buyers know what is being studied.

One high-tech research system is being operated in Williamsport, Pennsylvania, by Chicago-based Information Resources, Inc. The firm's "Shopper's Hotline" program gives participants the chance to win free trips and merchandise if they agree to use a special identification card when making purchases in local stores. When the card is run through the store's bar-code scanning equipment, a computer file on each participant's purchases is created which allows buying trends to be monitored.

Information Resources also uses the Williamsport cable-TV franchise to advertise products being offered on a trial basis and to test new commercials before they appear nationally. The market-research firm inserts its own commercials into network programming in place of commercials the rest of the country sees. Local viewers do not know which ads are being tested. It is also possible for certain commercials to be targeted to individual households. Using the demographic data obtained from Shopper's Hotline participants, a family that owns pets can be targeted for a pet-food commercial while a family with a personal computer can watch an ad for new software. A computer calls each of the three thousand participating households each night to link up with devices inside TV cable converters to determine what programs were watched that day. This information on the commercials viewed is correlated with data on what purchases were made in local stores provided by the bar-code scanning devices.

Federal law prohibits cable television companies from releasing information about an individual's viewing choices, retail purchases, or any other personally identifiable data without written or electronic consent. While there have been few state laws enacted in this area, in Connecticut it is illegal to install a monitoring device inside a residence without the cable subscriber's permission, to release subscriber lists without the opportunity for individuals to delete their names, or to disclose viewing habits without prior consent. California, Illinois, Wisconsin, and the District of Columbia have laws prohibiting electronic surveillance or monitoring by cable companies.

Electronic Mail

Another form of eavesdropping that may grow with the spread of technology is the interception of messages sent between computers. Electronic mail involves the sending of written messages between locations via computer networks and is becoming one of the important growth industries. Companies such as GTE, Telenet, and others have recently developed electronic mail services, and so have large corporations such as Citicorp for their own internal electronic mail systems. The Office of Technology Assessment recently reported that two-thirds of the Postal Service's 110 billion pieces of annual mail could be handled electronically.

Television Cameras

Technological advances have created television cameras that are small and light-sensitive as well as inexpensive enough to be used for secret surveillance in homes and offices. Most banks have TV cameras installed on their premises and on automatic teller machines to reduce theft and fraud. Frequently the customer is not aware that he is being photographed, but he is being observed, and his image is kept on file in a permanent record.

However, devices which are quite intrusive at times can prove to be helpful. In one such case, a man insisted to his bank that he had not made a transaction using his bank card. He was able to convince the bank only when a hidden camera revealed that a police officer had been the user of the bank customer's card. The officer had stolen the card and fraudulently used it. In another situation, a camera took the picture of a man who used a dead man's card. The user turned out to be the dead man's murderer.

List Compilers

List compilers hold important stores of personal information about us all. These were originally developed for direct-mail marketers, but have come to be used in many ways to make decisions about you and me, even by the Internal Revenue Service.

Your name on any of a number of lists could influence decisions concerning you without your knowledge. List compilers develop and make available to a variety of organizations the names and addresses of persons classified by them into specific profile groupings. These lists are developed by obtaining names and addresses from public records, such as automobile registrations and census tract data, and by renting lists from private firms, such as magazine and book publishers, credit card companies, and charitable or professional organizations. They are then combined into various configurations by computer to develop desired groups. The final profile lists are rented out to employers, business organizations, and government agencies, among others. You don't know what lists you are on, or how they are being used to make decisions about you.

At one point an Idaho-based neo-Nazi organization established a computer-based network to link extremist groups and to disseminate lists of those people that the organization said "have betrayed their race." One of the lists in the group's computer data bank was entitled "Know Your Enemy." It contained the names, addresses, and telephone numbers of "race traitors" and "informers." The computer link itself was called the "Aryan Liberty Network" and was sponsored by what the organization called the Aryan Nations. From its centralized data bank, any of its members wanting advice about "race traitors" could obtain appropriate guidance along with lists of "enemies."

Chapter 10, "Do You Know Where Your Name, Address, and Profile Are?," contains a full discussion about list compilers.

Sources of Personal Data

Consumer reporting organizations, credit card companies, and bank checking accounts are rich sources of personal information that is being stored in computer data banks. If you ever want to know a person really, find out how he spends his money. Things like the books and magazines he buys, the organizations he belongs to or contributes to, and where he travels tell a great deal about personality and life-style.

Information obtained from data compilers, legitimately or illegitimately, could dramatically affect how people interact with you. Even personal and sensitive items about you in the press, whether they are true or not, find their way into data-bank dossiers on you. Almost thirty years ago, the renowned journalist H. V. Kaltenborn, disturbed by tactics of overzealous reporters even then, wrote that such tactics expressed "one of the elements of our times, the indifference to personal privacy, the assumption that a free press means a licensed press and the fact that today there is too much privilege on the part of the reporter to invade the privacy, the decency, the self-respect of the individual who is being interviewed." With today's computers, the substance of unreasonably personal interviews, including exaggerated or even incorrect "facts," can become a permanent record available for distribution instantaneously throughout the world.

Devices to intrude on our personal privacy may come in many forms. A Utah dentist is marketing an identification system to help locate missing children. Dental records have long been a source of identification for police and forensic work, but this new procedure affixes a wafer with an identification number to a person's tooth. Each number is kept on file in a computer bank along with telephone numbers of persons to call in case of an emergency. A Miami plastic surgeon has patented a homing device which would be implanted behind a child's ear to help parents locate missing children. The device would emit a signal that could be monitored by a cellular telephone system or by satellite. The device could also be used to help police monitor parolees or aid in finding patients who wander away from institutions. Currently, private industry and government agencies have expressed interest in the invention. While such devices may prove very useful in locating missing persons and monitoring parolees, they also have larger implications for a society trying to protect individual freedom against abuses of privacy invasion by the government and others.

Our personal, sensitive information falls into many unintended hands in the normal course of activities. A doctor at Billings Hospital in Chicago counted the number of people with legitimate access to patients' records. He stopped his count when he reached seventy-five people. Many of these play no part in the patient's treatment. They include secretaries, file clerks, auditors, insurance company personnel, and other non-medical employees.

While individuals fight to view their own medical records, more outsiders are gaining easy access to patient files. Insurance companies, professional review organizations, and employers who administer their own health insurance programs are some of the third parties usually encountering little or no opposition when requesting to see medical records.

One reason the computer is causing such concern is that today as never before, decisions about a person are made based entirely on information in a record, rather than by face-to-face discussion. And that information is not always correct, timely, or relevant.

For example, in New Orleans a computer doing a routine background check on Shirley Jones, a woman applying to adopt an infant, revealed an arrest warrant for another woman of the same name. The innocent Jones was arrested twice, spent time in jail, and had three court appearances before the error was corrected.

Generally data entered into a data bank is never destroyed, and can haunt you the rest of your life. When errors occur, institutional procedures are not always adequate for making corrections.

To give us the kind of protections to help prevent abuses, we should have the right to see the personal information about us in an organization's records. We should be able to correct those records if they are in error. We should know who is keeping records about us, and why. We do not have those full rights.

In the latest Gallup poll on privacy, made several years ago, 47% of the people surveyed believed they had little or no privacy because the government could learn anything it wanted to know about them. An additional 19% said the likelihood of losing their privacy was very great. Thus a total of 66% of the respondents were concerned about their lack of personal privacy rights. A Lou Harris poll in 1983 disclosed that three-quarters of the participants were "very" or "somewhat" concerned about threats to personal privacy, an increase of 23% from a similar survey taken ten years earlier. The same survey also revealed that the respondents ranked privacy high among problems to be confronted in the year 2001. Yet, our nation's highest tribunals are slow to respond. "The time to guard against tyranny," Thomas Jefferson warned, "is before it shall have gotten hold of us." Former President Lyndon B. Johnson counseled, "For centuries the law of trespass protected a man's lands and his home. But in this age of advanced technology, thick walls and locked doors cannot guard our privacy or safeguard our personal freedom. Today we need a strong law—suited to modern conditions. . . ." Yet, he did not have such a law enacted during his administration.

Conclusion

Encroachment on personal privacy is an increasingly important issue facing the individual today. Personal information is collected for specific purposes, and later often combined with additional information. The compiled data is then available to an ever-increasing number of institutions and may be used for a multitude of constructive purposes, but it has been known to be abused. Records greatly influence one's life. There is a large margin for error when one realizes that information collected from unquestioned sources often is entered into data banks without verification for accuracy. Innocent errors are disseminated, at times to the detriment of the subject.

Improvements in computer technology also have opened the door to sophisticated computer crime. Computers give the criminal relatively easy access where intrusion is virtually undetectable. Data can be altered, leaving no audit trail.

It is clear that individual privacy rights are slipping away. Laws are beginning to recognize the right to information privacy, but more is needed. Of equal importance is the need for the people to be fully aware of the ever-increasing computer intrusions on our personal lives.

3

What's in Your "Confidential" Personnel File and Who Sees It?

We should keep in mind that the humanities come before the dollars. Our first duty runs to man before business, but we must not forget that sometimes the two are interchangeable.

—*Bernard M. Baruch*

A reputation once broken may possibly be repaired, but the world will always keep their eyes on the spot where the crack was.

—*Joseph Hall*

A candidate for a key job in a corporation located in the Southwest was passed over because his personnel file included the phrase, "has larcenous tendencies." His original file had been improperly summarized, and investigation showed that a prank played in the ninth grade had been the basis of the damning phrase.

In another case, a Chicago woman who had been turned down for several government jobs found that the reason stemmed from a note in her grammar school records. Her third-grade teacher carelessly wrote on a report that the woman's mother was crazy. This casually written notation was now in the woman's computerized file.

These people were unaware that there was anything of that nature in their files until they each took legal action to demand to know the true basis for an unexpected adverse decision, and in so doing got access to their records. If they had had the foresight to look into their files before reports were ordered by the decision makers, at least explanations could have been entered into the records and the shattering outcomes might have been averted.

Your employer keeps all kinds of information about you in his files, much of it instantaneously retrievable. Do you know what that information reveals about your life? Who else sees it, and what do they do with it?

As recently as the mid-fifties, most employers collected only a limited amount of information about their employees. For the most part, standard payroll records and time cards were sufficient to meet internal needs and fulfill government data requirements. All of this has changed. Federal agencies and departments, such as the Equal Employment Opportunity Commission (EEOC), the Occupational Safety and Health Administration (OSHA), the Department of Health and Human Services, the Labor and Defense departments, and law enforcement agencies are making substantial demands on employers for information about their individual employees. State and local government units add to the stream of personal data that has to be collected.

At the same time, in administering increased and varying employee benefits, employers gain access to private and sometimes extremely sensitive information, not only about employees, but about their families as well. Long- and short-term disability funds, sickness and accident plans, pension and life insurance benefits, and educational assistance programs all require additional record keeping by the employer. Company medical departments often have individual files of their own, supplementing standard personnel records. The knowledge available to an employer about an employee's affairs extends well beyond traditional job-related data.

Even when a person applies for work today, it is not unusual for the employer to request a considerable amount of personal information about the applicant and his family. The employer then goes about verifying and supplementing it. In addition, the job applicant probably will be examined by the company doctor, interviewed in depth, given a battery of psychological and aptitude tests, and subjected to a background investigation by an outside investigative firm. If he gets the job, his records will further expand to accommodate attendance and payroll data, benefits data, performance evaluations, and a mass of other information. The total information base created through this process is often viewed as a valuable resource by parties outside the employer-employee relationship.

Under the existing system, a person does not know what is in his record and therefore cannot protect himself against the use of poor-quality information by those who make decisions. In most cases where a person is turned down for a job, the applicant is never given the true reason. In those cases where an explanation may be required, it is only given if the individual specifically requests it. The average person is either unaware of this right, or discouraged by the inconvenient and time-consuming procedures he must go through to get the information. The rejected applicant is more apt to reason that it is easier to forget about the unpleasant experience and apply someplace else, never realizing that the information on which he was turned down is now part of his file, a file that could be repeatedly copied and distributed in the future.

In the small organization, employee information is usually kept in one file, with the file's custodian performing a variety of loosely related record-keeping functions. In the large organization, the employer must deal in a consistent way with a great many employees and must match job requirements to individual abilities. This calls for specialized functions and records. Over the years, personnel departments have expanded to handle not only recruitment, selection, and job placement, but also, in many cases, industrial relations, benefit programs, medical programs, and compliance with government requirements.

Ready access to large amounts of stored information tends to create an incentive to use that information for marginal and intrusive purposes.

It is virtually impossible to state with certainty that a particular adverse employment decision was based on a record. Unlike insurance, credit, or medical decisions, crucial employment decisions do not always come directly from recorded information. However, the close relationship between employee records and the decision-making process is clear.

Inevitable Abuses and Hardships

It is thus not surprising that numerous privacy problems develop throughout the system and that all too often, individuals are harmed in the process. One technique which gives rise to abuse is the use of the pretext interview. In such interviews, investigative firms making employee background checks encourage agents to misrepresent themselves and the reason for the interview in order to elicit candid information from others.

It is common practice for many employers to use private agencies to check employee or job applicant backgrounds. In their investigative capacity, agents talk with neighbors, business colleagues, associates, former employers, and former teachers, then submit their reports which, unverified, tend to be only as reliable as the informant or the individual making the check.

In some cases, individuals are victimized by unreasonable decisions triggered by computer-stored information. In one case, a seventeen-year-old girl was denied a job as a clerk in a large department store because a computer revealed that she had been caught shoplifting when she was twelve years old. Even though she had not been arrested or convicted, and although there was some doubt concerning the identity of the shoplifter, the fact that the incident was part of the record without explanation labeled her a security risk.

An area receiving the increasing attention of labor unions is the use of automated systems for employee surveillance in the workplace, an uncharted legal area. Monitoring the speed and efficiency of employees with computers is beginning to supplement and even replace surveillance with video cameras. A system which is installed without restraining controls enables supervisors and coworkers to snoop into employees' work lives.

The Right to Know Why

Adverse decisions against an individual may be made for any number of reasons, most of them valid and logical, but some may be based on false or obsolete information. The collection and use of outdated, adverse personal information unrelated to qualifications for a job may stigmatize the individual far into the future. For such a person, the ability to find and hold gainful employment is a critical factor. The process of selection among job applicants generally involves a step-by-step disqualification of candidates based on negative information. Where jobs require routine skills, or where many apply for a few vacancies, items of information bearing little or no connection to the job qualifications tend to become the basis for elimination. Thus, an old arrest record, a less-than-honorable military discharge, or a childhood prank, however remote from the needs of a particular job, often becomes the rejecting factor. This, of course, is both a disservice to the individual and a loss to society.

When background checks on executives and other key personnel are involved, privacy invasion may go to such extremes as the bugging of rooms and recording of telephone conversations. According to one report, an applicant for an executive position was so disturbed by the secretive manner in which his prospective employer, a Connecticut manufacturer, investigated him by calling his golf club and making inquiries about his wife that he declined the job when it was offered.

Adverse information—distorted or not—in the files of investigative agencies serving employers could have disturbing consequences. In one case, a bright, ambitious, junior executive in his thirties had a promising career ahead. A challenging advancement opened up, the kind of opportunity he had been hoping for. What's more, no one in his organization was more qualified for the promotion, and he was the logical choice. It was an important policy-making position, and the company routinely ran a full background check on all applicants for that level of executive by engaging an outside investigative firm. The young man was neither consulted nor advised of this action.

The report that came back branded him as having a questionable character and as being an undesirable risk in a top management position, despite the fact that for the past eight years, the frivolities and adventuresomeness of youth behind him, he had been a model employee who made substantial contributions to his company. The reason for this adverse report went back to the time he had tried smoking marijuana as a youth, and a neighbor had mentioned the incident to an insurance investigator. That, coupled with wildly exaggerated accounts in the record of the few visits he and his wife made to a psychiatrist early in their marriage to help resolve passing marital difficulties, was enough to deny him the job. It mattered little that he had not used any drugs or visited a psychiatrist for many years. The information was still in the computer data bank. Had the junior executive been permitted to learn what was in his computer file before any decision was made, he would have had the opportunity to supplement that record with a full explanation. Perhaps the final outcome would have been different.

In another case, the time had arrived when John, the executive vice-president who had devoted his twenty-year career to the company, expected to be appointed president. The incumbent president was retiring in four months and a committee of the board of directors had been designated to formally make the recommendation for his successor. To the shock of John and his colleagues, when the announcement was officially made, the selection turned out to be the second vice-president, a man with far fewer credentials and less time with the company.

All explanations by the board spokesperson rang hollow, and John was determined to get the full story. He hired a lawyer who subpoenaed the files of the selection committee. Those files revealed a complete copy of his medical records maintained by his personal physician. In his physician's scrawled handwriting was the notation, "patient seems to have trouble managing his finances." The notation was made at a time when John was having persistent headaches and his doctor was probing all possible causes, including mental pressures.

The selection committee of the board of directors of the company, studying that notation, reasoned that if the executive vice-president could not manage his own finances, they could not risk recommending him for the presidency where he would have to manage the finances of the company. If John had not insisted on learning the full facts and backed that insistence with expenditures for legal counsel, he never would have learned that the casual notation by the physician contributed to the devastating result. Although too late to prevent the harm already done, now at least he was able to explain and correct the record to avoid additional damage in the future.

Confidentiality: The Stamp and the Reality

A spokesperson for the Oil, Chemical and Atomic Workers International Union, commenting on breaches of confidentiality in the handling of insurance claims, raised some disquieting points when he stated, ". . . the doctor fills out the claim form. The claim form goes to the insurer. The insurer submits it in most instances to company claim departments. I have had complaints where someone, a secretary in an office, will say, 'Gee, Jane Doe really had a great time on that cruise three months ago because I have a claim form for an abortion here.' You get that because someone in that personnel department is given the responsibility of going over claim forms."

An employee availing himself of medical services offered by his employer does so at some risk to the traditional confidential relationship between physician and patient, unless great care is taken to insulate that relationship from the usual work-related responsibilities of the medical department.

Corporate physicians are sincerely concerned about possible misuses of the records they maintain. But no matter how hard they strive to be independent, their allegiance is ultimately to the employer. Some large employers have procedures that guarantee the confidentiality of medical record information in all but the most extreme circumstances; and many corporate medical departments only make recommendations for work restrictions, carefully refraining from passing along any diagnosis or treatment details in all but the most urgent cases. Nevertheless, it is the corporate doctor's duty to tell his employer when he finds in an individual a condition that could adversely affect the interests of the employer or other employees.

In one case, a researcher conducted a study on the smoking habits of employees in a manufacturing plant. Employees were told the project was one of several, and they willingly cooperated by disclosing how many cigarettes they smoked each day. When the survey was completed, and the results announced, the nonsmoker manager was surprised to learn the large number of employees who smoked two or more packs a day. He prevailed on the researcher to allow him to see the individual names of these employees. With that list in hand, during the next several months the manager proceeded to move in subtle ways to remove and/or demote the two-pack-a-day workers.

Although a person may have difficulty seeing his or her own medical records, notations in a patient's medical file are hardly confidential. Aside from investigating agencies who obtain "confidential" medical records for a fee, medical information is routinely made available to inspection bureaus, centralized data banks, auditors, and a variety of investigators assigned to preparing reports. In addition, such information is seen by secretaries, file clerks, health insurance company personnel, as well as nurses and physicians in the course of their routine work. A physician in a New York hospital found that there were thirty-five people who had access to a patient's medical files who did not render any medical treatment.

Security records differ from the usual personnel records in that they are often created without the employee's knowledge. Sometimes the information in them is inconclusive, or the problem that precipitated the record is not quickly resolved. Nonetheless, an employer may have to keep security records to safeguard the workplace or corporate assets. Security departments traditionally cooperate with personnel departments in investigating incidents involving employees. Where the security and personnel functions are separate, however, security records are often filed by incident and not by individual. Since these records have little, if any, impact on personnel decisions about an employee, giving supervisors or employees free access to them might be difficult to justify. But where security records are used for discipline, termination, promotion, or evaluation, fairness dictates that the employee be made cognizant of the file and given the opportunity to challenge, correct, or add his own comments to it.

In practice, information flows freely among employers, personnel managers having their own rather close-knit fraternity. In addition, it is not uncommon for some supervisors to bypass the personnel departments altogether in checking on an applicant by directly contacting the candidate's former supervisor. The employee has no way of knowing this is going on.

Legislative and Regulatory Intervention

Frequent and extended interactions between personnel and government inspectors, auditors, and contract monitors make it likely that more records will be required in the years ahead to support an even larger range of federal, state, and local government and management decisions. Some legislation enacted for the benefit of employees may now be creating opportunities for abuse of privacy rights. The Employee Retirement Income Security Act (ERISA), for example, underscores the increasing importance of the employer's role as provider of social and economic benefits. Yet neither the actual requirements imposed by such legislation nor regulations issued to implement it account for its overall impact on the collection, use, and disclosure of the employee information it generates. State laws also have had an impact upon the collection of information about employees and, most particularly, about job applicants.

The Equal Employment Opportunity Commission does not require employers to create or maintain any specific records on individuals. But in order to demonstrate compliance with its statutorily defined objectives, employers necessarily must create more elaborate records. If an affirmative action program is required, as under the Rehabilitation Act or the Age Discrimination Employment Act, or is voluntarily undertaken out of a sense of corporate responsibility, records are essential.

The Occupational Safety and Health Act (OSHA) has created more than ordinary concern with regard to what constitutes fair and proper information practices. With reference to specific health hazards, it provides in part that

OSHA "shall prescribe the type and frequency of medical examinations or other tests which shall be made available by the employer at his cost, to employees exposed to such hazards." Results of the examinations or tests may be given to a prospective employer if the employee authorizes it. This raises the possibility of an individual's medical records following him from job to job. Some workers already have declined to take employer-advocated physical examinations for fear of the consequences of having a disability documented in their records.

Voluntary Constructive Activities

Several of the nation's largest and most progressive corporations now have voluntarily initiated information policies designed to ensure the privacy and confidentiality of employee records to the maximum degree possible. The International Business Machines Corporation believes its concerns about privacy make good business sense because initiatives in this area have improved employee relations. The quantity of data in the company's personnel files has been pared to a minimum. Such personal data as payroll deductions, life insurance, home ownership, mortgages, and wage garnishments are classified as "non-worker-related" and are not available even to supervisory people. Information dealing with arrests and convictions is used for security purposes only.

IBM keeps its files as current as possible. Data concerning training grades and conviction records are destroyed after three years. Any employee is provided on request with a computer printout of his file. With regard to medical records, employees have full access to information kept for government requirements or concerning voluntarily requested examinations. Doctors' notes, however, are only reviewed with the employee by the doctor. Where outside inquiries are made, IBM will only verify employment and will not release salary or performance data without the employee's written consent. If personal information is requested by a law enforcement agency, an individual determination on compliance is made in each case.

At the Equitable Life Assurance Society, where a major restructuring of personnel policies took place, only nine items are included in the personnel files. These include only job-related material, such as employment applications, leave of absence requests, and salary actions.

At Bank of America, giving employees access rights to their personnel files is part of the firm's stated employee relations policy. It is convinced that openness is the best way to instill employee confidence.

Citibank voluntarily adopted fair information practices for all its personnel records. As a result, the vice-president in charge of that function at the time of the adoption stated that the efficiency of the operations of the personnel department was improved, and the costs reduced. All extraneous data previously accumulated in individual personnel files were removed and irrelevant information is no longer being collected.

In the early part of the twentieth century, personal information sought by private business may have been more intrusive than it is today, but it was generally used only by the particular employer. There were no computer data banks to store the information indefinitely and it could not be instantly retrieved or transmitted around the world.

At that time, the Ford Motor Company had a sociological department with one hundred investigators who would go into the workers' homes to make sure that no one was drinking too much, that their sex lives were unblemished, that houses were clean, and that off-work hours were spent profitably. Workers found wanting were fired from the high-paying jobs of $5.00 a day. Employment applications in those days asked such questions as: Do you smoke? Do you gamble? Do you swear or use slang? Who is your political leader? Have you been divorced?

Today, the modern Ford Motor Company is in the forefront of practicing exemplary employee privacy protection policies. The policies, all contained in company manuals, include five basic "Fair Information Practice Principles":

1. There shall be no personal data record-keeping system whose existence is secret.
2. There must be a way for an individual to find out what information about him is in a record and how it is used. With a few exceptions—such as security clearance data, and certain testing and evaluation material to determine qualifications for appointment or promotion—employees are permitted access to their records.
3. There must be a way to prevent information obtained for one purpose from being used for another purpose without employee consent. The only information given to a prospective employer on a former employee is his dates of employment, last position held, final base pay, and whether or not he is eligible for re-employment.
4. An employee must be permitted to correct or amend records about him. Ford Company personnel are urged to keep all personal data current, and are encouraged to advise the company of educational progress and the like which could affect their potential for future promotions. In addition, the program permits salaried employees to enter into their personnel files statements of their interest in specific positions and/or developmental opportunities, looking toward fuller utilization of their capabilities.
5. Any organization maintaining, using, or disseminating personal data must assure the reliability of the data and take precautions to prevent its misuse.

Unfortunately, the number of companies with such wholesome guidelines represent a limited number of the total work force in America. Thousands of other large, medium, and small organizations employing many millions of people have not yet responded.

The survey of Fortune 500 companies reported in Chapter 4 revealed that 80% of the companies disclosed personal information to credit grantors, 58% to landlords, and 25% to charitable organizations. Yet, three out of five did not have a policy to inform their employees of the routine disclosure practices to nongovernmental inquirers. As a matter of fact, almost 60% do not even inform their personnel of the records kept about them or how they are used. One-third of the companies get information from third parties without obtaining written permission from the employee or applicants.

"Nothing But the Truth"

The Roman philosopher Epictetus once wrote, "Liars are the cause of all the sins and crimes in the world." Some managements appear to take this sentiment seriously. Companies large and small use polygraphs at some time, including the voice-stress analyzers that measure changes in microtremors of the voice. Historically, retailers have been the users of the lie detector, but now the equipment is used in almost every industry. Today, private sector firms alone administer as many as 2 million polygraph tests each year. This is three times the number of tests conducted just ten years ago.

Our survey detailed in the following chapter found that 15 percent of the nation's largest corporations used polygraph or other truth-verification equipment to verify information about personnel. Ninety-five percent of those used it "under circumstances of possible theft or sabotage" and only 10 percent for "screening of applicants."

By far, the great majority of polygraph users do so in an effort to cut employee theft losses. "The average merchant," stated a Montgomery Ward Company spokesperson, "does not recognize that he loses more to employees than to others. From 50 to 70 percent of our loss goes to employees, and this is the same for any retailer. Shoplifters don't take you for nearly as much."

Employee theft is the largest single category of nonviolent crime committed against business and costs business an estimated $40 billion a year, according to the American Management Association, with most of the loss being passed on to the consumers in the form of higher prices. The U.S. Department of Commerce has estimated that employee theft causes as much as 20 percent of the nation's business failures. University of Minnesota researchers recently found that approximately one-third of the employees in retail department stores, hospitals, and electronics manufacturing firms reported some involvement in workplace theft.

In administering polygraph tests, blood pressure tubes are attached to the subject's arm and chest and electrodes placed on his fingers. Then, the person is asked a series of questions while his emotional response is registered by pen and ink on a paper roll. Physical changes recorded during the test include alterations in blood pressure, pulse rate, and respiration that may occur when a person lies. A negative result on the test, measured by irregular marks on the paper, may not mean that the subject is guilty. Some people's inherent nervousness causes recordings that resemble those made when lying. Others are able to consistently pass such a test even when not telling the truth.

Many pharmacy chains use polygraph tests to learn whether job applicants have been past drug abusers, claiming that these people are more likely to steal on the job. Here are some other ways polygraph testing is being used:

- A corporation based in Florida spent $500,000 in one year to polygraph employees in its 800-unit chain. At some time in his employment, everyone in the company, including the president, has to take the test.
- In Maryland, a manufacturer was so eager to reduce theft that it offered employees a profit-sharing plan in return for their submission to Psychological Stress Evaluator (PSE) tests. The workers accepted.
- In Massachusetts, a company uses PSE tests on tape recordings it routinely makes of auto insurance claims. In about 20 percent of the tests, which were conducted on "suspicious" claims and usually without the claimants' knowledge, the analyzers had detected stress that led to further investigation and sufficient evidence to deny fraudulent claims.
- A Georgia nursing home used polygraphs to screen out potentially sadistic or disturbed nurses and orderlies.
- In Florida, department store officials tested every employee who had access to the store safe in an effort to recover $500 that was missing. The store's assistant manager flunked two polygraph tests and was fired. Later another man who had passed the lie detector test was found to be the culprit.
- A nationwide chain of jewelry stores does periodic polygraph examinations and pre-employment polygraph examinations. The chain's internal security department also uses this procedure for investigating in-store thefts. During the investigation employees are forced to pass along gossip and hearsay regarding other employees or be fired.

We are faced with a conflict of values. No reputable citizen would deny the employer's right to aggressively protect his assets and expose employee dishonesty. Nor would any informed individual dispute the economic reality that employee theft boosts the selling price of merchandise. Many employers claim the polygraph is a necessary tool for the good of society. On the other hand, the arguments against polygraphs concern the ways they are used, their margin for error, and the unfair interpretations that may result from the findings.

In one highly publicized case, a major union representing striking employees charged that professional polygraph test operators who screened job applicants for their client asked such questions as: Did you ever commit a crime for which you were never convicted? Do you change your underwear daily? Have you ever done anything with your wife that could be considered immoral? Have you ever had extramarital sex relations? Are you a Communist?

Executives of the client company asserted they did not know such questions were on the tests, which were prepared by the outside polygraph operators. When the company officials were informed, they ordered such questions dropped. The union wanted the company to stop using polygraphs entirely. It refused to do so.

A union official related the following experience which he characterized as a "polygraph horror story":

> We had a fellow who was working last year in Ohio, where he was a member of our local. There occurred a $1,000 shortage. The company security urged every-one to take a lie detector test. Our people told the members not to take the test. The employee, however, was vehement. He felt he was innocent, and he volun-teered. . . .
>
> Now, deep down inside, in his subconscious, he was convinced that the shortage occurred outside the store somewhere after the money left the store and before it got to the bank. When the polygraph operator was rattling off a series of questions, he suddenly asked, "Do you know who took the money?" And [the employee] hesitated, of course, he didn't know; but there was a suspicion in the back of his mind, and he answered that he had no idea.
>
> The polygraph caught the hesitation and recorded it. He was immediately sus-pended, lost his job. [The local] then filed a grievance. There was no settlement at either step 1 or step 2 of the grievance procedure, but finally the union repre-sentative settled the case with the company personnel manager. [The man] was reinstated with full back pay, no loss of seniority, and returned to his same job classification. That is a happy ending, but that is because he had an aggressive and militant union willing and able to defend his rights. That is not the case across the country, and this is what concerns us very clearly. That is why we think a federal law is necessary.

Many people believe polygraph tests are invasions of privacy because examiners ask sensitive personal questions, the answers to which find their way into personnel files, with employment decisions ultimately made on what may be unreliable information. In practice, there is no such thing as a voluntary lie detector test. If a job applicant refuses to submit to a lie detector exam-ination, what chance does he have of even being considered for employment? Thus, it is argued that the use of the polygraph for screening job applicants by a company is coercive.

An Army study concluded that the accuracy rate of polygraph examinations is 76%. When the U.S. Privacy Protection Commission examined the use of the polygraph, witnesses indicated that accuracy ranged from 65% to 90%. David C. Raskin, professor of psychology at the University of Utah, who has done extensive work with polygraph examinations, explains this wide disparity. He believes the level of accuracy of the polygraph in employment-related uses suffers from the absence of a proper psychological atmosphere in pre-employment screening, the limited time devoted to this testing, and the very nature of such screening. He believes such testing should be banned in the private sector for screening and periodic testing.

On balance, it is fair to conclude that the use of polygraph testing to screen job applicants abuses a prospective employee's privacy rights. The questions asked may be unreasonably intrusive, and the polygraph device itself is not sufficiently reliable when used in the employment process. Recognizing this fact, on 27 June 1988 President Reagan signed into law the Employee Polygraph Protection Act of 1988 prohibiting the use of lie detectors by private companies in pre-employment screening and for random testing of employees. Only pharmaceutical companies and private security firms are exempt from the ban, and the administration of any lie detector test must conform to federal guidelines to insure accuracy and fairness. Incidentally, it is ironic that during face-to-face discussions, the interviewer can detect the truthfulness of responses 60 percent of the time by normal visual observations of physiological and other reactions.

Because lie detector tests and the devices themselves have been frequently criticized as being unreliable, their use is often avoided. An inaccurate result can mar a person's reputation for life. While lie detector tests have helped investigators in criminal cases, a 1983 study conducted by the Office of Technology Assessment concluded that the validity of polygraph tests in personnel security screening could not be asserted. And in a 1987 staff paper by the same agency it was suggested that there is no more reason for assuming the validity of polygraphs now than there was in 1983. Interestingly enough, in our survey, 32 percent of the Fortune 500 companies responding advocated that "more stringent personnel screening practices be used by the government as opposed to business in adopting programs for polygraph testing."

The American Psychological Association has adopted a resolution stating that scientific evidence on the effectiveness of polygraph or lie detector tests "is still unsatisfactory." A 1986 Media General–Associated Press poll indicated that a majority of Americans do not think lie detectors should be used by businesses to screen job applicants or current employees.

The Central Intelligence Agency and the National Security Agency both screen prospective job applicants and, on a periodic basis, test some of their nearly 100,000 current employees. From time to time there have been proposals for widespread testing of federal employees involved in national security matters, but in specific cases, polygraphs have been of little help in protecting the national interest. For example, in 1985 former CIA employee Larry Wu-Tai Chin was charged with spying for China for thirty years, yet passed lie detector tests several times.

If the polygraph raises citizen concern about privacy invasion, the voice-stress analyzer is even more suspect. Firms that sell the device claim guilt produces stress and the absence of stress is evidence of innocence. The degree of accuracy achieved, however, is debatable. Operators of voice-stress analyzers concede that the device does not work on psychopathic liars. Further, all agree that the test is no more efficient than the operator who administers it. A union official noted the device "beats Big Brother at its best, because there is no need to attach a person to a machine. All you need is a microphone."

Among other tests now being used is the chemical procedure called urinalysis. A recent survey of over 700 U.S. corporations, government agencies, and organizations found that over 200 of the firms had drug-testing programs. The study also found that 16 percent of employees not passing drug tests are subsequently fired. Those using urine tests to check for marijuana or drug use include police and fire departments, the Ford Motor Company, and the National Football League. This test is not always accurate, as Washington, D.C., officials found out a few years ago when they had to reinstate 24 of 39 police recruits suspended for the detection of drug use. Unfortunately for the 24 reinstated recruits, the city had already publicly announced them as marijuana users.

In his book *The Great Drug War* (1987), Dr. Arnold Trebach of American University in Washington, D.C., says that "approximately 5 million people were tested this year in America" for drug use. He further states that while drug-testing companies, such as Syva Company of Palo Alto—makers of the EMIT test—claim a 95 percent accuracy rate, the rate would be more like 90 percent when the tests are performed by people other than Syva's own technicians. According to Trebach, "If there were a false reading rate of 10 percent, with half false positives and half false negatives, this could mean that 5 percent of the approximately 5 million people tested this year in America were accused improperly of being drug users. Thus, there is a good chance that 250,000 employees were placed under suspicion or had their careers ruined for no reason."

According to Roger P. Maickel, Professor of Pharmacology and Toxicology at Purdue University, legitimate drugs and even some food components can result in false positives during urine testing. He asserts that a person could be exposed to substances in the atmosphere, such as marijuana, that might cause a test to be positive even though the person had never actually used the substance. "The personal, legal, and economic ramifications of this are mind-boggling," Maickel says. "There is the potential for thousands of people testing positive from urine tests. Additional data . . . confirmation that the individual is under the influence of a drug, or has purchased or used the drug . . . is essential."

According to the American Civil Liberties Union, the estimated five million people who went through urinalysis testing in 1985 included bus drivers, factory workers, nurses, drugstore clerks, utility workers, foremen, pilots, and most of the lower ranks of the armed forces and Coast Guard. The ACLU estimates that today the number of people being tested is "triple to quadruple that figure." As mentioned above, the University of Illinois survey revealed that 58 percent of the nation's largest employers have a drug-testing program.

In Milwaukee, school board members are considering altering school bus company contracts to make drug testing mandatory for bus drivers. Public awareness of the issue there was heightened when thirteen out of fifty-five drivers tested positive for marijuana and cocaine. Some bus company owners are supportive of mandatory testing, and some have called for legislative action by the state to require the tests for all bus drivers. In June 1987, the Wisconsin School Bus Association, made up of representatives from state bus companies and school districts, adopted a resolution supporting mandatory testing for all new drivers and for drivers renewing their licenses.

Interestingly enough in one case, an arbitrator ruled that Greyhound Bus Lines could not order drivers to stop using marijuana when not working, saying, "Workers in society are free men and women, with the fundamental right to live their lives as they choose." Greyhound argued that concern for the safety of its passengers outweighed the infringement on personal liberties.

Polygraph Restrictions

As observed above, the Employee Polygraph Protection Act of 1988 which became effective 27 December 1988 prohibits the use of lie detectors in pre-employment screening and for random testing of employees by private firms. Only pharmaceutical companies and firms employing security guards in areas related to "health and safety" are exempt from the ban. The federal law also establishes guidelines for the administration of lie detector tests which stipulate that each test be at least one and one half hours long and that examiners administer no more than five tests in one day. All test questions must be discussed with the subject in advance. Questions may not be altered during the exam. And questions on religious, political, or union affiliation are not allowed.

Statutes have been enacted by thirty-two states and the District of Columbia concerning the use of polygraphs in employment, ranging from a complete ban of the use of lie detector devices by public and private employers to a simple requirement that examiners be licensed.

Alaska, Connecticut, Delaware, Hawaii, Massachusetts, Oregon, Pennsylvania, Rhode Island, and Washington along with the District of Columbia prohibit the use of lie detector tests in private or public employment. Some of these states specifically exclude law enforcement officers, persons with access to narcotics and dangerous drugs, and persons in positions related to national security from this prohibition. California and Idaho prohibit the use of polygraphs by private employers.

Fourteen states (Iowa, Maryland, Massachusetts, Michigan, Minnesota, Montana, Nevada, New Jersey, Tennessee, Texas, Utah, Vermont, West Virginia, and Wisconsin) and the District of Columbia prohibit the use of polygraphs as a condition of employment. Employee consent is required and the use of test results is limited. Some of these states prescribe using a refusal to take such a test and alleged lying in a test as the sole grounds for discharge of an employee.

Arizona, New Mexico, and Vermont require the licensing of examiners. This license may be revoked if an examiner asks certain questions or fails to obtain the subject's prior consent. Questions concerning sexual activities, political affiliation, labor organizing, religion, and marriage are prohibited in nine states (Arizona, Georgia, Illinois, Nebraska, Nevada, New Mexico, Tennessee, Vermont, and Virginia).

Relevant New York law is limited to the prohibition of psychological stress evaluators in employment. Such tests are also illegal in Wisconsin. Obviously, laws throughout the nation governing employee privacy rights vary widely.

Employment Record Protections Provided by States

In regulating access to personnel records, some states grant employees a right of inspection and limit disclosure to third parties in various ways. California, Connecticut, Delaware, Maine, Michigan, Nevada, New Hampshire, Ohio, Oregon, Pennsylvania, Rhode Island, Washington, and Wisconsin require all public and private employers to permit their employees to inspect records and personnel files concerning themselves upon request. However, letters of recommendation and investigative reports specifically are excluded. Michigan and Oregon entitle employees to copy their complete records, while Ohio permits the copying of medical records compiled by an employer's agent.

New York and Iowa allow only limited disclosure of public employees' records with the consent of the employee. In North Carolina, limited information including name, age, date of employment, position, title, salary, and most recent promotion or demotion in state, county, and local employment records is available to anyone. All other information is confidential.

Only Hawaii, Maryland, and Massachusetts limit the scope of an employer's investigation of an applicant. Maryland prohibits inquiries concerning any psychological or psychiatric condition which does not bear a "direct, material, and timely relationship" to the applicant's ability to perform the job. Maryland and Massachusetts also prohibit the use of expunged criminal records, arrests without convictions, and certain misdemeanor convictions for purposes of employment. Hawaii limits the use of arrest and court records.

Conclusion

In an age of voluminous record keeping, abuses are inevitable. The unregulated use of methods such as pretext interviews, the inclusion of off-hand or un-substantiated remarks, the use of tests such as polygraphs, and the release of data to third parties can produce adverse results for the individual. Because of the capacity and convenience of computers, employers are able to retain in their records information that has no justification being in personnel records. Medical information in the possession of employers, because medical benefits are provided by the company, may be included in those records. Although some companies voluntarily have adopted fair employee privacy protection policies, many have not. A responsible employer limits data kept in personnel files, allows employees access to their own files, and limits third-party access. Policies vary widely on personnel information practices. Several states have enacted measures to protect individuals, but much more is needed.

4

How Your Employer Is Handling Your Personal Information
A Survey of Individual Privacy Protection in Big Business

A comprehensive survey was conducted at the University of Illinois to determine the extent to which the largest industrial corporations of America have policies safeguarding the personal information they collect and maintain about their employees, former employees, and applicants for employment.

A sample of 275 companies was selected from among the Fortune 500 corporations. One hundred twenty-six companies, or 46% representing over 3.7 million employees, responded to the sixteen-page questionnaire. Because major corporations are standard setters of business practices, the impact of the policies described in this chapter goes well beyond the Fortune 500 corporations.

The findings are presented here in two sections: Section 1, Executive Summary of Highlights, and Section 2, Highlights, Survey, and Recommended Fair Information Practices.

Section 1. Executive Summary of Highlights

A. Disclosures of Personal Employment Data

Almost two out of five (38%) corporations do not have a policy concerning which records are routinely disclosed to inquiries from government agencies.

Four out of five (80%) of the corporations responding disclose personal information to credit grantors. Over half (58%) give the data to landlords.

B. Individual Access

While most corporations (87%) give employees access to personnel records, only about one in four (27%) allows access to supervisors' records.

Four out of five corporations (77%) allow employees to place corrections in their personnel records, and nine in ten (87%) forward these corrections to anyone who received the incorrect information.

C. Informing the Individual

Four out of ten corporations inform personnel of the types of records maintained (43%), how they are used (41%), and what company disclosure practices are (42%).

Two of five (42%) of the corporations responding find it necessary to collect information without informing the individual.

Four out of five (78%) organizations check, verify, or supplement background information collected directly from personnel.

D. Authorizing Personal Data Collection

Eight out of ten (78%) companies obtain written permission from the individual when seeking information about him/her from a third party. In spite of this, one out of three (34%) does seek information from a third party without written permission.

When written permission is not obtained, most corporations do not have a policy of informing an individual of the types of information sought (71%), the techniques used to collect it (80%), or the sources (75%).

E. Medical Records

One-half (50%) of the companies use medical records about personnel in making employment-related decisions. One in five (19%) does not inform the employee of such use.

Two out of three (65%) of the companies responding have restrictions in regard to smoking, but in all cases (99%) such restrictions apply to places where smoking is allowed.

One of fifty (2%) companies shows in its personnel records whether an employee is a smoker or non-smoker.

F. Drug Testing

Over half (58%) of the corporations have a drug-testing program in operation. Nine out of ten (89%) use the program for pre-employment screening.

One quarter (22%) of the companies responding have a drug policy, but no testing program.

Nine out of ten (86%) had a drug-testing program for two years or less. All (97%) began the program because of general concern for the safety of employees.

None of the companies release the results of drug tests to outside organizations.

G. AIDS Testing

Three percent have an AIDS-testing program in operation, and it has been in operation for less than a year. None of the companies release results to outside organizations. Another five percent have an AIDS-testing policy, but no testing program.

Ninety-two percent have neither a policy nor a testing program, and it is not likely that they will institute an AIDS-testing program of some sort in the next two years. Yet, two of five companies (42%) believe that government, as opposed to business, should have more stringent AIDS-testing personnel-screening practices.

H. Polygraph Use

Eighty-five percent of the companies do not use the polygraph or other truth verification equipment. Practically all (95%) of the 15% that do use such equipment do so under circumstances of possible theft or shortage. One in three (32%) of the companies responding believes more stringent polygraph testing policies should be used by the government as opposed to business.

The main reasons most companies do not use polygraph testing are validity and reliability of the tests (43%) and moral or ethical implications of use (34%).

I. Use of Investigative Reporting Firms

Over half (57%) of the organizations responding retain the services of an investigative firm to collect or verify information concerning personnel. About one in five (19%) of these corporations does not review the operating policies and practices of the investigative firm.

J. Arrest, Conviction, and Security Records

Ninety-one percent of the companies do not require the collection of arrest records of personnel. Three out of five (57%) do not require information on convictions.

K. General Practices

Over half the companies (55%) have a policy for conducting periodic evaluations of their personnel record-keeping system, and within the past two years half (49%) of the respondents conducted a systematic evaluation of their existing personnel record-keeping practices with particular attention to confidentiality safeguards.

Almost three out of four (72%) companies have designated an executive-level person to be responsible for maintaining privacy safeguards in employment record-keeping practices.

Practically all (98%) of the companies utilize computer facilities for record keeping, and 97% of payroll records information, 94% of personnel records, and 56% of group insurance records are in a common data bank. No employment applications inquire about an applicant's sexual preference.

Section 2. Highlights, Survey, and Recommended Fair Information Practices

A. Disclosures of Personal Employment Data

Highlights

Almost two out of five (38%) corporations do not have a policy concerning which records are routinely disclosed to inquiries from government agencies.

Four out of five (80%) of the corporations responding disclose personal information to credit grantors. Over half (58%) give the data to landlords.

Survey

Note: Numbers in parentheses following the percentages are the numbers of corporations answering this specific question.

1a. Does your organization have a policy concerning which records will be routinely disclosed to inquiries from government agencies?

Yes	62%	(78)
No	38%	(47)

b. If so, does this policy include the requirement of a subpoena for disclosure of personnel records to government agencies?

Yes	62%	(48)
No	38%	(30)

c. If you require a subpoena, which of the following kinds of subpoenas are recognized for release of such information?

	Yes	
(1) Grand jury	89%	(39)
(2) Administrative	86%	(37)
(3) Legislative	76%	(32)
(4) Other	44%	(19)

2a. Does your organization always require a subpoena before releasing information to any nongovernment inquirer?

	Yes	29%	(36)
	No	71%	(90)

b. Does your organization disclose information to any of the following nongovernment inquirers without a subpoena?

	Yes	
(1) Landlords	58%	(52)
(2) Credit grantors	80%	(72)
(3) Charitable organizations	28%	(25)
(4) Other	33%	(29)

Recommended Fair Information Practices

An employer should limit external disclosures of information in records kept on individual employees, former employees, and applicants; it should also limit the internal use of such records.

B. Individual Access

Highlights

While most corporations (87%) give employees access to personnel records, only about one in four (27%) allows access to supervisors' records.

Four out of five corporations (77%) allow employees to place corrections in their personnel records, and nine in ten (87%) forward these corrections to anyone who received the incorrect information.

Survey

3a. Does your organization have a policy giving your personnel access to their:

	Yes	
(1) Supervisors' records?	27%	(33)
(2) Personnel office records?	87%	(110)

(3) Accounting office records?	27%	(32)
(4) Insurance records?	66%	(81)
(5) Security records?	23%	(24)
(6) Medical records?	64%	(78)

b. If so, can they copy these records?

	Yes	
(1) Supervisors' records	62%	(18)
(2) Personnel office records	76%	(77)
(3) Accounting office records	79%	(22)
(4) Insurance records	81%	(60)
(5) Security records	74%	(14)
(6) Medical records	74%	(52)

4a. Does your organization allow personnel to correct or amend any of their:

	Yes	
(1) Supervisors' records?	30%	(36)
(2) Personnel office records?	77%	(95)
(3) Accounting office records?	26%	(30)
(4) Insurance records?	54%	(65)
(5) Security records?	21%	(21)
(6) Medical records?	44%	(52)

b. If so, are these corrections or amendments forwarded to anyone who received incorrect information?

	Yes	
(1) Supervisors' records	79%	(26)
(2) Personnel office records	87%	(71)
(3) Accounting office records	89%	(24)
(4) Insurance records	86%	(51)
(5) Security records	90%	(17)
(6) Medical records	89%	(39)

5. Does your organization have a policy stating who is authorized, within the organization, to have access to personnel records?

Yes	No
81%	19%

Recommended Fair Information Practices

A. An employer should permit individual employees, former employees, and applicants to see, copy, correct, or amend the records maintained about them, except highly restricted security records, where necessary.

B. An employer should assure that the personnel and payroll records it maintains are available internally only to authorized users and on a need-to-know basis.

C. Informing the Individual

Highlights

Four out of ten corporations inform personnel of the types of records maintained (43%), how they are used (41%), and what company disclosure practices are (42%).

Two of five (42%) of the corporations responding find it necessary to collect information without informing the individual.

Four out of five (78%) organizations check, verify, or supplement background information collected directly from personnel.

Survey

6. Does your organization have a policy to inform personnel of:

    a. The types of records maintained on each individual?

       Yes

       43%   (52)

    b. The use of these records within the organization?

       Yes

       41%   (50)

    c. Which records the individual has access to?

       Yes

       62%   (76)

    d. Which records the individual does not have access to?

       Yes

       45%   (54)

    e. The organization's routine practices of disclosure to governmental inquirers?

       Yes

       42%   (49)

    f. The organization's routine practices of disclosure to nongovernmental inquirers?

       Yes

       43%   (52)

    g. Any special, non-routine disclosure to governmental inquirers?

       Yes

       26%   (28)

    h. Any special, non-routine disclosure to nongovernmental inquirers?

       Yes

       23%   (25)

7. Does your organization ever find it necessary to collect information without informing the individual?

Yes	42%	(51)
No	58%	(71)

8a. Does your organization ever check, verify, or supplement background information collected directly from personnel?

Yes	78%	(97)
No	22%	(28)

b. Is the individual who is the subject of a background check always notified before such information is collected?

Yes	66%	(64)
No	34%	(33)

c. Is the individual who is the subject of a background check always notified after such information is collected?

Yes	3%	(1)
No	97%	(33)

d. Does your organization have a policy allowing the individual to have access to the information collected during a background check?

Yes	44%	(42)
No	56%	(53)

e. Is there a policy which allows the individual to correct or amend this information?

Yes	70%	(30)
No	30%	(13)

Recommended Fair Information Practices

A. An employer, prior to collecting the type of information generally collected about an applicant, employee, or other individual in connection with an employment decision, should notify him/her as to:
(1) the types of information expected to be collected;
(2) the techniques that may be used to collect such information;
(3) the types of sources that are expected to be asked;
(4) the types of parties to whom and circumstances under which information about the individual may be disclosed without his authorization, and the types of information that may be disclosed;
(5) the procedures established by statute by which the individual may gain access to any resulting record about himself;
(6) the procedures whereby the individual may correct, amend, or dispute any resulting records about himself.

B. An employer should clearly inform all its applicants upon request, and all employees automatically, of the types of disclosures it may make of information in the records it maintains on them, including disclosures of directory information, and of its procedures for involving the individual in particular disclosures.

D. Authorizing Personal Data Collection

Highlights

Eight out of ten (78%) companies obtain written permission from the individual when seeking information about him/her from a third party. In spite of this, one out of three (34%) does seek information from a third party without written permission.

When written permission is not obtained, most corporations do not have a policy of informing an individual of the types of information sought (71%), the techniques used to collect it (83%), or the sources (75%).

Survey

9a. Does your organization obtain written permission from an employee or applicant when you seek information about him or her from a third party?

Yes	78%	(98)
No	22%	(28)

b. If so, does this permission indicate:

	Yes	
(1) The specific third party?	69%	(66)
(2) The nature of the information being sought?	93%	(90)
(3) The specific individuals in your organization who may receive this information?	44%	(42)
(4) The specific purpose for which the information will be used?	89%	(86)

10. Are there instances when your organization does not obtain written permission from an employee or applicant when you seek information from a third party?

Yes	34%	(33)
No	66%	(64)

11. In those instances when written permission is not obtained, does your organization have a policy of informing the individual of:

a. The types of information expected to be collected about him or her from third parties?

Yes	29%	(18)
No	71%	(44)

b. The techniques used to collect the information?

Yes	20%	(12)
No	80%	(49)

c. The sources such as employers, credit bureaus, or independent check guarantee services asked to supply the information?

Yes	25%	(15)
No	75%	(46)

Recommended Fair Information Practices

No employer should ask, require, or otherwise induce an applicant or employee to sign any statement authorizing any individual or institution to disclose information about him, or about any other individual, unless the statement is:

(1) in plain language;
(2) dated;
(3) specific as to the individuals and institutions he is authorizing to disclose information about him;
(4) specific as to the nature of the information he is authorizing to be disclosed;
(5) specific as to the individuals or institutions to whom he is authorizing information to be disclosed;
(6) specific as to the purpose(s) for which the information may be used;
(7) specific as to its expiration date, which should be for a reasonable period of time not to exceed one year.

E. Medical Records

Highlights

One-half (50%) of the companies use medical records about personnel in making employment-related decisions. One in five (19%) does not inform the employee of such use.

Two out of three (65%) of the companies responding have restrictions in regard to smoking, but in all cases (99%) such restrictions apply to places where smoking is allowed.

One of fifty (2%) companies shows in its personnel records whether an employee is a smoker or non-smoker.

Survey

12a. Does your organization provide a voluntary health-care program, such as HMO or Kaiser Plan, or auto, life, or health insurance for personnel?

	Yes	
(1) A health-care program	10%	(13)
(2) Insurance	5%	(6)

(3) Both	80%	(100)
(4) Neither	5%	(6)

b. Are employee medical records kept together with other personnel records?

Yes	8%	(10)
No	92%	(108)

c. Are medical records ever used in making employment-related decisions?

Yes	50%	(59)
No	50%	(60)

d. Is the employee always informed of such use?

Yes	81%	(46)
No	19%	(11)

13. Does your organization have any restrictions in regard to smoking?

Yes	65%	(82)
No	35%	(44)

14. Does the restriction apply to:

	Yes	
a. Places where smoking is allowed?	99%	(81)
b. Time of day when smoking is permitted?	2%	(2)

15. Does your employment application inquire whether the applicant smokes?

Yes	2%	(2)
No	98%	(122)

16. Do your personnel records contain information on whether the employee is a smoker or non-smoker?

Yes	2%	(3)
No	98%	(122)

Recommended Fair Information Practices

A. An employer that maintains an employment-related medical record about an individual should assure that no diagnostic or treatment information in any such record is made available for use in any employment decision. However, in certain limited circumstances, special medical information might be so used after informing the employee.

B. Upon request, an individual who is the subject of a medical record maintained by an employer, or another responsible person designated by the individual, should be allowed to have access to that medical record, including an opportunity to see and copy it. The employer may charge a reasonable fee for preparing and copying the record.

C. An employer should establish a procedure whereby an individual who is the subject of a medical record maintained by the employer can request correction or amendment of the record.

F. Drug Testing

Highlights

Over half (58%) of the corporations have a drug-testing program in operation. Nine out of ten (89%) use the program for pre-employment screening.

One quarter (22%) of the companies responding have a drug policy, but no testing program.

Nine out of ten (86%) had a drug-testing program for two years or less. All (97%) began the program because of general concern for the safety of employees. None of the companies release the results of drug tests to outside organizations.

Survey

17a. Would you describe your organization as having:

	Yes	
(1) A drug-testing program in operation?	58%	(73)
(2) A drug policy, but no testing program?	22%	(28)
(3) Neither a policy nor a testing program?	20%	(25)

 b. If you have a drug-testing program, does your organization conduct drug tests for:

(1) Pre-employment screening of applicants?	89%	(65)
(2) Probable cause following employee accidents?	75%	(55)
(3) Employee tests at annual physicals?	16%	(12)
(4) Random employee tests?	12%	(9)
(5) Tests of known past users?	29%	(21)

18. Does your organization release the results of drug tests to outside organizations?

Yes	0%	(0)
No	100%	(74)

19. How many times during 1986 was drug testing used at your organization?

Range	Mean (average)	Median (middle number)
0–10,000+	772	100

20. For which of the following reasons did your organization begin a drug-testing program?

	Yes	
a. Because of incidents and/or drug use on the job	69%	(50)
b. Because of general concern for safety of employees	97%	(70)
c. In response to government regulations	10%	(7)

d. To follow the lead of other organizations	21%	(15)
e. To try to keep health-care costs down	51%	(37)
f. To allow enforcement of company drug policies	40%	(29)
g. To improve your company's public image	22%	(16)

21. How long has your organization had a drug-testing program? Would you say:

a. Less than 1 year	42%	(30)
b. One to two years	44%	(32)
c. Over two years	14%	(10)

22. Would you say the overall reaction of employee unions to your drug-testing program is:

a. Very positive	4%	(2)
b. Positive	41%	(17)
c. Mixed	47%	(26)
d. Negative	18%	(10)
e. Very negative	—	—
f. Not applicable	—	(10)
g. Don't know	—	(8)

23a. What are the positive effects that resulted from your organization's drug-testing program?

(1) Screen applicants	26%	(20)
(2) Safer workplace	25%	(19)
(3) Less health care	16%	(12)
(4) Increased awareness	9%	(7)
(5) Care given	5%	(4)
(6) Improved company image	5%	(4)
(7) Decreased absenteeism	4%	(3)
(8) Company claims down	3%	(2)
(9) Increased productivity	3%	(2)
(10) Other	4%	(3)

b. What are the negative effects?

(1) None	30%	(17)
(2) Adverse effect	25%	(14)
(3) Costs	14%	(8)
(4) Privacy invaded	13%	(7)
(5) Union opposition	7%	(4)
(6) Test unreliable	7%	(4)

24. If you do not have a drug-testing program, on a scale of 1 to 10, with 1 being very likely and 10 being not very likely, what is the likelihood that your organization will institute such a program in the next 2 years?

	Range	Mean	Median
	1–10	6.6	7.1

Recommended Fair Information Practices
See Section E, Medical Records.

G. AIDS Testing

Highlights

Three percent have an AIDS-testing program in operation, and it has been in operation for less than a year. None of the companies release results to outside organizations. Another five percent have an AIDS-testing policy, but no testing program.

Ninety-two percent have neither a policy nor a testing program, and its not likely that they will institute an AIDS-testing program of some sort in the next two years. Yet, two of five companies (42%) believe that government, as opposed to business, should have more stringent AIDS-testing personnel-screening practices.

Survey

25a. Would you describe your organization as having:

	Yes	
(1) An AIDS-testing program in operation?	3%	(4)
(2) An AIDS-testing policy, but no testing program?	5%	(6)
(3) Neither a policy nor a testing program?	92%	(113)

  b. If you have an AIDS-testing program, does your organization conduct AIDS tests as part of:

	Yes	
(1) Pre-employment screening of applicants?	75%	(3)
(2) Employee tests during annual physicals?	75%	(3)
(3) Random employee health tests?	25%	(1)

26. Does your organization release the results of AIDS tests to outside organizations?

Yes	0%	(0)
No	100%	(4)

27. How long has your organization had an AIDS-testing program? Would you say:

a. Less than 1 year	75%	(3)
b. One to two years	0	(0)
c. Over two years	0	(0)

28. Would you say the overall reaction of employee unions to your AIDS-testing program is:

		Yes	
a.	Mixed	25%	(1)
b.	Not applicable	75%	(3)

29. On a scale of 1 to 10, with 1 being very likely and 10 being not very likely, what is the likelihood that your organization will institute an AIDS-testing program of some sort in the next 2 years?

Range	Mean	Median
0–10	8.0	8.9

Recommended Fair Information Practices
See Section E, Medical Records.

H. Polygraph Use

Highlights

Eighty-five percent of the companies do not use the polygraph or other truth-verification equipment. Practically all (95%) of the 15% that do use such equipment do so under circumstances of possible theft or shortage. One in three (32%) of the companies responding believes more stringent polygraph testing policies should be used by the government as opposed to business.

The main reasons most companies do not use polygraph testing are validity and reliability of the tests (43%) and moral or ethical implications of use (34%).

Survey

30a. Does your organization ever use polygraph or other truth-verification equipment to verify information about personnel?

	Yes	15%	(19)
	No	85%	(106)

b. If so, is the polygraph used in:

(1) Screening of applicants?	10%	(2)
(2) Periodic checks of all employees?	5%	(1)
(3) Checks of particular types of employees or individuals?	16%	(3)
(4) Under circumstances of possible theft or shortage?	95%	(18)

c. How many times during 1986 was the polygraph used?

Range	Mean	Median
0–50	6	3

31. What procedures are used in addition to polygraph or similar testing for personnel selection?
    a. Personal interview   100%   (18)
    b. Traditional reference check   89%   (16)
    c. Psychological testing   17%   (3)
    d. Credit check   44%   (8)
    e. Police-record check   44%   (8)

32. What procedures are used in lieu of polygraph or similar testing for personnel selection?
    a. Personal interview   96% (103)
    b. Traditional reference check   95% (102)
    c. Psychological testing   13%   (14)
    d. Credit check   14%   (15)
    e. Police-record check   18%   (19)

33. What is the main reason that your organization does not use polygraph testing?
    a. Cost as compared to other selection methods   7%   (7)
    b. Speed of obtaining results   2%   (2)
    c. Availability of trained operators   6%   (6)
    d. Validity and reliability of the tests   43%   (45)
    e. Moral or ethical implications of use   34%   (36)
    f. Other   28%   (30)

34. What is the main reason that your organization uses polygraph testing?
    a. Cost as compared to other selection methods   6%   (1)
    b. Speed of obtaining results   0%   (0)
    c. Availability of trained operators   6%   (1)
    d. Validity and reliability of the tests   39%   (7)
    e. Moral or ethical implications of use   6%   (1)
    f. Other   39%   (7)

35. What is your estimate of the percentage of firms within your own industry using the polygraph or similar tests in personnel-related areas?

Range	Mean	Median
0–100	12%	5%

Recommended Fair Information Practices

An employer should not use a polygraph or other truth-verification equipment to gather information from an applicant or employee.

I. Use of Investigative Firms

Highlights

Over half (57%) of the organizations responding retain the services of an investigative firm to collect or verify information concerning personnel. About one in five (19%) of these corporations does not review the operating policies and practices of the investigative firm.

Survey

36a. Does your organization ever retain the services of an investigative firm to collect or verify information concerning personnel?

Yes	57%	(55)
No	43%	(41)

b. Does your organization review the operating policies and practices of the investigative firm?

Yes	81%	(43)
No	19%	(10)

c. How often?

Monthly	0%	(0)
Semi-annually	5%	(2)
Yearly	32%	(12)
Other	63%	(23)

Recommended Fair Information Practices

Each employer and agent of an employer should exercise reasonable care in the selection and use of investigative organizations so as to assure that the collection, maintenance, use, and disclosure practices of such organizations fully protect the rights of the subject being investigated.

J. Arrest, Conviction, and Security Records

Highlights

Ninety-one percent of the companies do not require the collection of arrest records of personnel. Three out of five (57%) do not require information on convictions.

Survey

37a. Does your organization have a policy requiring that information concerning arrest records of personnel be collected?

Yes	9%	(11)
No	91%	(115)

b. If so, is the collection of this information required by federal, state, or local law?

	Yes	10%	(1)
	No	90%	(9)

c. Is this information ever removed from individual personnel records?

	Yes	20%	(2)
	No	80%	(8)

38a. Does your organization have a policy requiring that information pertaining to a conviction of any employee be collected?

	Yes	43%	(54)
	No	57%	(71)

b. If so, is this information collected from all personnel?

	Yes	88%	(46)
	No	12%	(6)

c. Is information concerning all types of convictions collected?

	Yes	47%	(24)
	No	53%	(27)

d. Is this information updated at set intervals?

	Yes	12%	(6)
	No	88%	(45)

e. Is the collection of this information required by federal, state, or local law?

	Yes	14%	(7)
	No	86%	(43)

39. Are security records, that is, records compiled during a security investigation of personnel, kept together with other personnel records?

	Yes	15%	(19)
	No	55%	(69)

Recommended Fair Information Practices

A. When an arrest record is lawfully sought or used by an employer to make a specific decision about an applicant or employee, the employer should not maintain the record for a period longer than specifically required by law, if any, or unless there is an outstanding indictment.

B. Unless otherwise required by law, an employer should seek or use a conviction record pertaining to an individual applicant or employee only when the record is directly relevant to a specific employment decision affecting the individual.

C. Except as specifically required by federal or state statute or regulation, or by municipal ordinance or regulation, an employer should not seek or use a record of arrest pertaining to an individual applicant or employee.

D. Where conviction information is collected, it should be maintained separately from other individually identifiable employment records so that it will not be available to persons who have no need of it.
E. An employer should maintain security records apart from other records.

K. General Practices

Highlights

Over half the companies (55%) have a policy for conducting periodic evaluations of their personnel record-keeping systems, and within the past two years half (49%) of the respondents conducted a systematic evaluation of their existing personnel record-keeping practices with particular attention to confidentiality safeguards.

Almost three out of four (72%) companies have designated an executive-level person to be responsible for maintaining privacy safeguards in employment record-keeping practices.

Practically all (98%) of the companies utilize computer facilities for record keeping. Of those, 97% of payroll records information, 94% of personnel records, and 56% of group insurance records are in a common data bank. No employment applications inquire about an applicant's sexual preference.

Survey

40a. Does your organization have a policy for conducting evaluations of its personnel record-keeping system?

Yes	55%	(69)
No	45%	(57)

b. Does your organization designate an executive-level person to be responsible for maintaining privacy safeguards in employment record-keeping practices?

Yes	72%	(89)
No	28%	(35)

41. Within the past two years, has your organization conducted an evaluation of its existing personnel record-keeping practices with particular attention to confidentiality safeguards?

Yes	49%	(62)
No	51%	(64)

42. If yes, were any of the following items or procedures reviewed during this examination?

a. The types of records kept	100%	(62)
b. Importance of the information	90%	(55)
c. Use of records by different departments	92%	(56)

    d. Disclosure of information to outside sources   92%   (57)
    e. Informing employees on disclosures of this
       information   34%   (43)

43a. Does your organization utilize computer facilities for record keeping?

		Yes	98%	(123)
		No	2%	(3)

  b. If so, which of the following records are computerized?

	Yes	
(1) Personnel records	90%	(111)
(2) Payroll records	99%	(121)
(3) Security records	15%	(16)
(4) Employee medical records	34%	(41)
(5) Group insurance records	83%	(100)

  c. Are any of these records kept together in one common data bank?

	Yes	54%	(66)
	No	46%	(57)

  d. Which records are kept together?

(1) Personnel records	94%	(62)
(2) Payroll records	97%	(64)
(3) Security records	3%	(2)
(4) Employee medical records	14%	(9)
(5) Group insurance records	56%	(37)

44. Do your applications inquire about an applicant's sexual preference (i.e., homosexuality or heterosexuality)?

	Yes	0%	(0)
	No	100%	(126)

45. Should more stringent personnel-screening practices be used by the government as opposed to business in adopting programs:

a. For polygraph testing?	32%	(29)
b. For drug testing?	50%	(51)
c. For AIDS testing?	42%	(42)

Recommended Fair Information Practices

An employer should periodically and systematically examine its employment and personnel record-keeping practices, including a review of:
    (1) the number and types of records it maintains on individual employees, former employees, and applicants;
    (2) the items of information contained in each type of employment record it maintains;
    (3) the uses made of the items of information in each type of record;

(4) the uses made of such records within the employing organization;
(5) the disclosures made of such records to parties outside the employing organization;
(6) the extent to which individual employees, former employees, and applicants are both aware and systematically informed of the uses and disclosures that are made of information in the records kept about them.

Conclusion

The policies and methods used by an employer to manage the personal information files of employees can have a significant impact on the lives of those employees. Often information of a personal nature is collected and included along with pertinent personnel data. Employees may not be aware of the types of data collected, methods of collection, or the sources consulted. Even medical information and sometimes the results of drug testing are included. Employees are, in many instances, denied access to all or portions of their own files while the employer may release the same information to third parties. Employees who are allowed access to files may not be allowed to correct errors in the information.

Business decisions such as hiring and promotion are sometimes made on the basis of information that should never have been included in the file. A totally unsubstantiated negative item can result in a tarnished career. Release of this kind of information to third parties could compound the damage.

Although employers may be aware that tight policies regarding personal files are needed, not much has changed during the past decade. More constructive action by employers is needed to fully protect the employees' privacy rights.

5

Business and Computer Privacy

Nobody ever pries into another man's concerns, but with a design, or to be able to
do him a mischief.

—Robert Smith

A man identifying himself as a banker called the Federal Reserve Bank in
Minneapolis, Minnesota, with instructions to transfer $16,255 electronically
from the Aberdeen National Bank in South Dakota to an account at the Citizens
and Southern National Bank in Atlanta. He supplied the day's code word,
and a routine transfer was made. Six months later an embarrassed Federal
Reserve official admitted that the caller, an ex-convict, had learned enough
about the Federal Reserve's codes to fool the system with ease.

An employee of a Maryland computer company that maintained classified
government files dialed the company's telephone number from his home in
Virginia, and by entering secret passwords into a terminal hooked up to his
telephone, he tapped into its computer. He extracted forty rolls of computer
printouts before he was caught.

The potential for unauthorized, undetected access to computerized company
records makes it impossible for knowledgeable executives or their professional
advisors to assure themselves or the groups they serve that their records have
not been manipulated, not just from within a business enterprise or from next
door but from any place on our satellite-encircled globe. The sophistication
of this new frontier of white-collar crime borders on the exotic. For example,
seven New Jersey youths, all under the age of eighteen with such code names
as Beowulf, Vampire, Treasure Chest, and Red Barchetta, in July 1985 were
charged with intruding into credit company computers and using other people's
credit cards to order merchandise for themselves, making free long distance
telephone calls, and accessing the coded Defense Department communications
system. It was even alleged by Middlesex County, New Jersey, Prosecutor

Alan A. Rockoff that they obtained codes to cause communications satellites to change position. In another case, in Oregon, an eighteen-year-old used a remote terminal to take control of the Department of Motor Vehicles' electronic system located in Salem, Oregon. He then deliberately put the system into total and irreversible disarray to illustrate its vulnerability.

Recently young West German hackers accessed at least twenty computers in the U.S. space agency and claim to have had the capability to paralyze the entire computer network of the National Aeronautics and Space Administration (NASA). Over 1,600 computers in nine countries are linked by the system, including those at the atomic research facility at Los Alamos, New Mexico. According to news reports, these young people may have obtained secret data on U.S. space projects, including the space shuttle and rocket failures. The hackers cited "unbelievable weaknesses" in the network's security system that allowed their exploits to occur.

In 1986, a study conducted by the Office of Technology Assessment revealed that while much attention is focused upon computer thieves who operate from outside the target information system, in many cases more significant security problems are posed by individuals authorized to use the system. The government-wide National Telecommunications and Information Security Committee also observed that the majority of crimes against government computers were committed by persons working with those same computer systems.

Values that free enterprise stands for—confidentiality, fairness, unintrusiveness, and unrestricted business entrepreneurship—are being compromised by electronic advances now sweeping society. Unfortunately, business and government mores, many auditing procedures as well as laws, provide inadequate protections of these values.

Telecommunications and satellites are being used in the normal course of business today by major corporations and banking institutions to transmit business records from one part of the nation and world to another. State and national boundaries have no significance with this electronic magic and therefore are essentially ignored.

The data speeding through space are the ingredients from which managements mold their services to customers and all of society. Yet, they are subject to unauthorized electronic access which leaves no trace. In spite of recently enacted computer crime laws, business organizations valuing the security of their records and other business information are finding it difficult, if not impossible, to protect data from persons with ulterior motives.

When I chaired the U.S. Privacy Protection Commission as it began its hearings about a decade ago, most of the executives from many of the nation's leading corporations who were called to testify before us were skeptical of the need to be concerned about abuse of personal and business data in their data banks. Their general attitude was, "We are not abusing anybody's information privacy and no one is abusing my privacy. Commission, you are wasting your time." Even a member of the Privacy Commission from industry, at the outset of the commission's deliberations, expressed doubts about the need for concern for privacy abuses in industry. It is a tribute to him that after several months of hearings, he became one of the staunch proponents for establishing privacy protection procedures in industry, including his own.

Senior corporate executives who appeared as witnesses, after hearing testimony from abused witnesses and after being questioned extensively by the commissioners, also changed their reactions dramatically. The typical changed reaction was, "We never thought about the issue that way. It could be a major problem. You may be assured of our full cooperation. If my company can help you in your important work we will be pleased to volunteer our facilities and services."

Data in computers are vulnerable to removal and manipulation in ways unheard of during the "file cabinet" era. Business executives in particular should be alert to this significant potential for damage. Too many are not. These are some of the questions executives should ask themselves: Do we know whether anyone has obtained unauthorized access to our computers, since there are no trails and science has not yet developed the technology to assure the prevention of unauthorized access? What will happen to the personal, sensitive information about us in our company files when we are no longer executives there? In view of the increasing frequency of business takeovers by foreign interests, who will control our company, and therefore all its sensitive information about its executives and customers next year, and what will they do with that information?

Technological Advances Continue

Every five or six years in its short history of approximately forty years, a new generation of computer components and equipment has appeared, increasing processing speed and reliability while reducing physical size and cost. For example, a computer that cost $1 million in the 1950s and occupied an entire room now costs less than $20 and is a postage-stamp-size silicon chip that is over 100,000 times faster. Work that required twenty-four hours then is now done in less than a minute.

Even the most powerful computer in existence is ultimately dependent upon fallible human beings for its input. Although computer crimes make headlines, simple errors and omissions throughout the data life cycle are responsible for the vast majority of data problems, creating such consumer headaches as mistaken identification, incorrect ineligibility determinations for certain programs and benefits, and difficulties in establishing and settling computer-billed amounts. Estimates have attributed 50 percent of computer-related losses to human errors.

Because of their great speed, computers pose the risk of making the identical errors thousands of times in a very short period. Besides the mere repetition of errors, a multiplying effect may result from one error triggering a series of errors. Nevertheless, systems security expert Royal P. Fisher recommends businesses concentrate on controlling basic accesses to their systems by advising them to "close the doors and windows before worrying about the cracks in the walls."

Once an organization establishes computer and telecommunications facilities, there is no technological means of preventing their use for other purposes. This includes fraudulent use of computer time and storage capacity. For example, two New York Institute of Technology personnel used the school's computer to run a data-processing business on the side. The corporation they established provided electronic data-processing (EDP) operations for a medical magazine subscription company, an import-export dealer, and an aircraft parts concern. It was discovered because the wrong-doers became too ambitious. The school officers' suspicions were aroused when the computer ran twenty-four hours a day but produced less work. Grade records, mail, and daily processing were delayed.

Business leaders and governmental officials are just beginning to grasp what these technological developments mean to their institutions. A survey of one hundred companies by Price Waterhouse and Company revealed that only one out of five (19%) of the companies provides guidance for data-security controls for microcomputers that can tie into the company's main computer. About half (52%) have policies concerning general use of microcomputers. Nearly six out of every ten company microcomputers tie into another computer system within or outside the company. A spokesperson for Price Waterhouse said they found situations where controllers can manipulate accounts receivable data and where company employees can mistakenly erase mainframe data.

Traditional protections for restricting incoming or outgoing information are ineffective. Information needed to conduct commercial and governmental affairs is also news for newspapers or other media. Often the same information is used by subversive groups. Corporate executives or incumbent government officials feeling the least bit insecure because of aggressive competitors, internal agitators, or abusive neighbors are justified in feeling vulnerable. No corporation, or for that matter no nation, is secure if it cannot protect itself against eavesdropping and other intrusions.

The Concerns of Nations

Many nations are convinced that their interests are being threatened by telecommunications and computer technology because of their increasing dependence on those corporations and nations with the most sophisticated scientific capability. In Sweden, for example, in the past the fire department had inventoried all buildings and had put the data into a computer so that when a building was on fire, the relevant fire station could communicate with the computer to determine the nature of the contents of the building. The computer data bank that contained the records of the contents of those business establishments in Sweden was located in the United States.

This situation and other developments motivated the Swedes to undertake a long-range look at the problem of computer vulnerability. A Vulnerability Board was appointed by the Swedish government in 1981. Several years later the board reported that the computerization of society had continued at an undiminished rate without adequate resources being assigned for security and reduced vulnerability. The report contained a plea for more analysis and education about the vulnerability problem and vigorous action to raise the consciousness of computer users everywhere.

Canada believes the transfer of business records out of the country for processing by United States corporations raises questions of property, economics, and security. The one-way southward flow of Canadian records to the United States for collating, classification, and analysis is seen as competing not only with Canadian industries but also with Canada's sovereignty and with the free flow of information at both the domestic and international levels. The loss in foreign exchange to Canada to pay for this service at one time was projected to reach $1 billion. Job losses to the Canadian economy were estimated to run as high as forty thousand. Concern had reached such proportions that a Canadian newspaper speculated that, unless Canada insisted that its computerized information remain within its own borders, the United States might eventually own all of Canada's secrets.

At an international conference of delegates representing twelve industrialized nations in which I represented the United States in 1980, the French delegates took the position that informational transactions are now an important part of international trade, yet they are not subject to a tariff. Further, they argued that the processing of business and governmental records abroad replaced French workers whose earnings were subject to their income taxes. France proposed developing a taxing mechanism on information that flowed into and out of that country. Such tariffs or other data restrictions, of course, could create chaos in multinational business affairs.

The economic interests of corporations and nations are being subjected to the dominance and control of organizations possessing superior technical equipment and know-how. For example, originally established by NASA and now owned and operated by Earth Observation Satellite Co. (jointly owned by Hughes Aircraft Company and RCA Corporation), there exists a remote sensing photo-satellite system called LANDSAT. From over ten thousand miles up in the sky, this facility obtains data from which analysts are able to determine the natural resources deep in the ground under someone else's property. This information is being collected from all over the world.

Not infrequently organizations engaging in this kind of remote sensing or those taking advantage of LANDSAT's findings may have better information about the natural resources of a corporation or a nation than do the landowners themselves.

Airline systems in all countries of the world often find it necessary or desirable for operational purposes to ignore political boundaries. This includes Iron Curtain countries. Domestic airlines in Poland, Czechoslovakia, and Hungary along with many of the other European and African nations maintain computer data banks in Atlanta, Georgia.

The transfer of information in and out of a nation without the knowledge of the authorities in the jurisdiction raises a number of issues that in years before the communications revolution were barely perceptible, if they existed at all. Increasingly, many sites are becoming transfer stations for business information records. Whose laws have jurisdiction when records are in a country only for processing or even for retransmission? If data are transmitted by a Polish national by way of an American satellite to a British corporation, whose laws control, and when? Is a satellite over twenty thousand miles up in the sky and jointly owned by American, British, and French interests within the jurisdiction of the American judicial system?

Many corporations and business associations disturbed by the conditions that presently exist in the international area have been trying to stimulate action leading to a solution. In January 1985, the Business Roundtable, an association of leading business executives, adopted a plan for action, suggesting principles to be included in an international information flow agreement. The list of principles was prefaced with:

> In the past fifteen years, the flow of information across national borders has increased dramatically. Multinational corporations have a growing dependence on international information flow, including everything from internal corporation information transfers to trade in information-based products and services.

> An increase in barriers to the free flow of information has caused increased concern within the business community. The problem does not affect only the service and high-technology industries. It affects any company using telecommunications internally or to serve its customers.

> *No internationally accepted principles currently govern the treatment of international information flow. Individual national policies are at best confusing, and at worst conflicting.*

Information privacy issues in the workplace were addressed ten years ago when the Business Roundtable adopted "A Policy Paper Regarding the Issue of Privacy in the Employment Setting" with the release of its *Fair Information Practices: A Time for Action.* The Business Roundtable believes that the free flow of information between nations advances the human condition and enhances both national economies and the world economy. While supportive of the social objectives of privacy and data protection, it urges governments to minimize the economic side effects of these laws. Expressing the belief that taxation of trade in information services is not practical or conducive to overall economic growth, the policy paper states that information cannot and should not be treated as a traditional commodity.

On 11 April 1985 the Organization for Economic Cooperation and Development (OECD) ministers adopted the OECD Declaration on Transborder Data Flows (TDF), indicating their commitment to address economic issues raised by the "information revolution." This document declares member nations' intentions to:

1. provide access to data and information and related services, and avoid the creation of unjustified barriers to the international exchange of data and information;
2. seek regulations and policies relating to information, computer, and communications services affecting TDF;
3. develop common approaches for dealing with issues related to TDF and, when appropriate, develop harmonized solutions;
4. consider possible implications for other countries when dealing with issues related to TDF.

At the same time, the declaration acknowledges that the ability of member countries to reap benefits from TDF may vary, that national policies affecting TDF reflect a range of social and economic goals, and that governments may adopt different means to achieve their policy goals.

This language understates the break separating the United States and other exporters of services who desire a liberal international environment for the services trade, and developing countries opposing such efforts in fear that the growth in their own data services industry would be hindered.

Hans Peter Gassman of the OECD has observed that electronic linkage of economic information is causing a growing apprehension among the publics of all nations concerning the erosion of economic independence. Linkage permits the extended control of the information environment and of records of business entities.

An international computerized banking system called SWIFT—the Society for World Financial Information Transactions—has been developed to permit banks on a worldwide basis to make loans almost instantaneously without transferring any currencies. Hundreds of thousands of transactions can be handled at a time, and because of speed, it operates essentially without national monitoring and often without internal controls. In effect, a form of stateless currency is created by juggling massive sums of money through the sky, creating the potential for accounting manipulation and damage to international financial markets.

It should be noted, however, that transborder data-flow when properly constrained is highly beneficial to all parties. It facilitates the integration of world markets and the flow of cross-national information, goods, and services.

Many nations including Sweden, West Germany, France, and the Netherlands already have legislation in an attempt to maintain control over information within their borders. It is not only business and government enterprises that are affected by such barriers. Consumers ultimately pay for costs resulting from decreased efficiency, lower productivity, and greater outlays for equipment and services. The nature of electronic data, however, makes such legislative action rather ineffective. Data move from country to country over various routes, depending on the availability of computer time and open telecommunications facilities.

In Britain, the Thatcher government has recently taken steps to combat high-tech computer fraud. Legislation has been proposed that would allow court witnesses to testify via a live video hookup. Under the Criminal Justice Bill, the statements of witnesses and other evidence could be used from other countries for cases involving international theft. Proponents of the bill view it as one method of matching the sophisticated tools of the criminal that allow the instantaneous transfer of money across international boundaries. The new procedures would also cut down on the expense of prosecuting a case in which all the witnesses and evidence were overseas.

The need for a more comprehensive response to data protection needs in this country continues to concern many United States trading partners and multinational corporations. Meanwhile, nations playing key global roles are working hard to try to top America's and the USSR's present technological superiority by applying more and more of their resources to this effort. A knowledgeable British observer, Anthony Smith, is convinced that the kind of scramble for communication media that has been under way in the industrialized world is on a scale similar to the first arms race in the postwar era. The United States is at economic and technological war with the rest of the world, he argues, and we are not even aware of it.

Computer Crime

"A product of the electronic revolution, the computer criminal strikes anywhere and everywhere. He is not a product of our slums; his clothing is usually the best; and his schooling, the finest. He represents the criminal of the future. Our laws are challenged by him, and our jurists are left stunned. What makes this criminal more dangerous than any before him is that, should our system of laws fail to meet his threat, he may, in fact, ring the death knell of our entire system of justice. The stakes are high indeed," says attorney August

Bequai in his book *Computer Crime*, published in 1978 and still relevant today.

One of the technical aspects that makes computer crime difficult to deal with is that clever, criminal-minded personnel are able to convert the operational advantages of the dramatically stepped-up information-processing pace to systematically manipulate accounts. For example, electronic technology permitted a $21.3 million embezzlement scheme at the Wells Fargo Bank in California. The bank's system of internal controls, which may have been adequate for less sophisticated systems, apparently was wholly inadequate for present-day instantaneous recording and transferring of funds. The fraud was uncovered only because the perpetrator carelessly filled out the wrong side of an entry ticket. The fraud was so simple to carry out that it reportedly took the embezzler only ten minutes every five days.

A recent American Bar Association survey of 283 large companies found that 48 percent of the firms had been victimized by computer criminals resulting in losses ranging from $145 to $730 million.

Technology permits major manipulations from sites far removed from clients' premises—even from distant parts of the world by use of satellites. Some electronics engineers hold that any hobbyist or amateur radio enthusiast can readily assemble the electronics needed to tune in to a computer from down the street. A $500 investment in equipment can give anyone in a van parked along the curb the ability to read off information appearing on computer screens in offices several stories above the street, and more sensitive equipment can pick off computer data from two kilometers away.

Computer Crime Has Several Faces

There is no generally accepted definition of "computer crime." In its 1986 report *Computer-Related Crime: Analysis of Legal Policy*, the Organization for Economic Cooperation and Development lists five basic types of computer crime. They include:

1. The input, alteration, erasure and/or suppression of computer data and/or computer programs done willfully, with the intent to commit an illegal transfer of funds or another thing of value.
2. The input, alteration, erasure and/or suppression of computer data and/or computer programs done willfully, with the intent to commit a forgery.
3. The input, alteration, erasure and/or suppression of computer data and/or computer programs, or other interference with computer systems, done willfully with the intent to hinder the functioning of a computer and/or telecommunications system.
4. The infringement of the exclusive right of the owner of a protected computer program, with the intent to exploit the program commercially and put it on the market.

5. The access to or interception of a computer and/or telecommunications system made knowingly and without the authorization of the person responsible for the system, either by infringing on security measures or with any other dishonest or harmful intent.

In his book *The Computer and the Law* (1984), Irving J. Sloan describes computer-related crime as involving "any illegal act for which knowledge of computer technology is essential for successful prosecution." This broad definition includes activities which potentially damage any entity that uses or is affected by computers and data communications systems, and persons about whom data are stored and processed in computers.

One approach which has been used is to classify computer crimes by the part the computer plays as the object, as the subject, as the instrument, or as the symbol. The nature of the "computer crime" generally determines which, if any, laws might apply.

Cases involving computers as the *object* of criminal activity include the theft or destruction of computers or of data or programs contained in them, or the destruction of vital support facilities such as air conditioning and electricity. Examples include such actions of student activists who in 1970 bombed the University of Wisconsin Mathematics Research Center, killing a physics researcher and costing over $18 million through the destruction of equipment and buildings, and the loss of accumulated data.

French computer installations at multinational companies in the past have come under terrorist attacks of bombing and sabotage. Heavy police protection had to be used to guard the computer facilities. One French electronics company had been accused of being "a salesman of electronic death" and was singled out because of its subsidiaries in Chile and Argentina. What do top executives do when centralized computer data banks containing all their organization's records are destroyed by such terrorist attacks in our unstable world? Should multinational corporations have duplicate data banks in another country? This may be the eventual solution.

Software and data have also been the object of theft and vandalism. Computer operators at *Encyclopedia Britannica* copied tapes containing two million customers' names and addresses which they sold to a direct-mail company. Fortunately, the tapes were recovered before they were used by competitors, averting a potential loss estimated at over $3 million. There have also been cases in which a company's financial records in the form of computer tapes and disks were stolen in order to extort ransom from their rightful owner.

Other threats to computer security that might be mentioned here are caused by accidents and acts of nature. These range from such minor instances as a dog chewing through a vital cable, to the computer and communications systems being damaged or entirely destroyed by earthquake, fire, explosion, flood, or blackout.

Most risks of computer manipulation can be avoided by designing appropriate systems. Obviously, those responsible must take the initiative to provide such systems. It should be noted that the foregoing kinds of computer crimes are those most amenable to effective prosecution under existing laws, and therefore can be dealt with more readily.

It is also feasible to take legal action against crimes where a computer is the *subject* of criminal activity. This involves those occasions when the computer is the site or environment of a crime, or the source of or reason for unique forms and kinds of assets.

Credit card fraud and theft from automatic teller machines (ATMs) are crimes directed against a computer itself. Other examples include commuters cheating computerized ticket dispensers in Paris and San Francisco, and theft from "smart" soft drink and refreshment machines.

These activities are largely due to some people's apparent dislike and distrust of computers in certain situations, and the age-old desire to "get away with something." As such, these consumer reactions are foreseeable, and appropriate safeguards can and should be built into a system's design.

Because these activities are effectively prosecuted under traditional laws, when a wrongdoer is apprehended, courts willingly interpret the action as being against the owner/operator of the machine.

Such is not the case where crimes involve unique assets created or compiled by a computer. Electronic Funds Transfer (EFT) systems are payment systems in which the exchange of value or money is represented by electronic messages. The ability to fraudulently appropriate funds is not unique to EFT systems, but the speed with which the money is transferred, allowing withdrawal prior to validation at the bank involved in a transaction, makes this type of crime troublesome.

From another dimension, vast amounts of personal data exist for the sole reason that computers can compile and store such information inexpensively. Sufficient safeguards must be instituted to ensure that personal information is not used for inappropriate purposes. An example of such misuse relates to airline computer data banks containing the names of people traveling together, places of travel, and reconfirmation telephone numbers or addresses at destinations. Such information could be seriously abused for business purposes, especially in times of intense rivalry. For example, in the mining industry, it has been known for one mining company to improperly learn the flight destinations of a competitor's geologists and other scientists in order to track where they might be conducting explorations for minerals. Where a person traveled yesterday or even a year ago, and with whom, and whose telephone number he or she gave for reconfirmation purposes could not only be embarrassing personally but even catastrophic to an executive's business interests or career.

A senior executive of one of the largest airlines in the world observed that before the installation of computers, reservations records were destroyed every ninety days. Since computers were installed several years earlier, none of those records had been destroyed.

The most common role played by the computer in illicit activity, and the most difficult to deal with, is when the computer is used as the *instrument* for the crime. A computer can be used either actively, as when automatically scanning telephone codes or gaining access to other information, or passively, to assist in simulation when planning an intended crime.

The direct object of these crimes is not always money. In one incident, a criminal diverted 217 railroad boxcars to a deserted stretch of track where they were emptied of their contents. In another case, a computer operator diverted $20 million worth of oil from a refinery to a barge waiting nearby.

Another disturbing type of development is the case mentioned earlier that involved students who infiltrated the University of Southern California's computer system, altered grades, and created fraudulent degrees which they sold for as much as $25,000. There is concern among educators and law enforcement officials that computer tampering could replace diploma mills and unaccredited offshore schools as the easy way to obtain a degree.

Techniques of the Computer Criminal

Automated systems can be compromised in various ways, each with its own terminology:

- *Electronic piggybacking* involves bypassing automated electronic identification verification controls within the computer system.
- *Impersonation* is the assumption of an authorized system user's identity. This is done by using another's I.D. card or passkey, or by electronically accessing a terminal with another's password.
- *Data diddling*, one of the common methods used in computer-related crime, is the changing of data either in the input or output stages.
- *Superzapping* involves the use of a universal access program, which is designed as a "master key" to bypass normal controls in cases of emergency. Such utility programs are powerful tools that should be kept secure from unauthorized use.
- *Trapdoors* are built into systems by designers to allow them simplified access. Frequently, subsequent operators neglect to eliminate or change these passwords. The leader of a group of teenage hackers testified, "If they had just changed those [passwords], we couldn't have gotten in."
- A *Trojan horse* involves the covert insertion of instructions in a program so that the computer will perform unauthorized functions, usually while still

performing its authorized tasks. In the form of a "logic bomb," unauthorized acts are executed at predetermined times or under certain conditions. In one case, a logic bomb had the following effect. On a specified day, two years after the crime was committed, at 3:00 p.m. a confession to the crime was printed on each of the victim company's three hundred terminals, followed by a systems crash. Of course, when this occurred, the perpetrator was a great distance away from the computer and its users.

• The *salami technique* is based on the belief that the appropriation of very small slices will not visibly reduce the whole. An example of this technique would involve the theft of small amounts from a great number of bank accounts, assuming that the individual depositors will not notice or complain about the small discrepancy.

Risk Reduction, Not Elimination

No computer system can ever be risk-free if for no other reason than its ultimate reliance upon humans who are error-prone, fallible, and amenable to corruption.

Particular problems are experienced by consumer-service institutions such as banks, which must provide security without unduly adding cost or inconveniencing customers. A spokesman for Chase Manhattan Bank characterized it as "a trade-off between security and a user-friendly system that does what we need it to do." Critics have charged that Chase Manhattan's system allowing pervasive access at all levels creates a situation where their computer is too "abuser-friendly."

Some banks and other institutions are attempting to improve their systems through the development of an electronic equivalent of the signature card, and encryption devices which scramble data. The development of such protections may involve considerable expense, but experience has shown that institutions that cannot afford adequate security measures cannot afford to operate a computer system.

In an effort to stop computer crime, law enforcement officials in Santa Clara County, California, in 1983 joined with private industry in a unique effort called DATTA—the District Attorney's Technology Theft Association. DATTA computer-crime specialists work with both police investigators and corporate security managers to solve computer fraud, chip theft, or trade-secret violations. DATTA has been involved in the specialized training of Federal agents, including FBI, Customs and Commerce investigators, and looks forward to expand its current data base system into a nationwide high-tech crime information clearinghouse.

In an attempt to identify and screen out potential systems abusers a business may use personnel practices that adversely affect the personal privacy rights of the individuals concerned. Such practices include overly extensive pre-employment background checks, loyalty oaths, and periodic polygraphing. Critics of these practices argue that the emphasis should be on incorporating effective security measures into employee training and in the design of personnel operations.

During the training period, employees should be educated in the need for, and methods to ensure, security. Stressing good housekeeping, internal controls, and personnel security practices minimizes the risk of inadvertent or even deliberate disclosure, alteration, or destruction of data. Periodic performance evaluations and salary incentives to reward employee security consciousness can be effectively utilized.

Internal controls can be effected by segregating the responsibilities of employees. Programmers should not concurrently act as computer operators. Access to computers should only be on a need-to-know basis. Employees should be required to take vacations. It is during periods that the regular operator is away from his duties that irregular practices and discrepancies frequently surface.

Most important, institute a policy of identifying and prosecuting computer criminals and strictly enforce it. Much computer crime, especially white-collar crime, goes unreported and unprosecuted. Such an environment is no aid to deterrence of criminal activity.

Status of Privacy Laws

Although the Privacy Act of 1974 set up certain safeguards against the misuse of federal records, there is limited federal protection from abuse of private sector records in the act. When I presented the report of the U.S. Privacy Commission, *Personal Privacy in an Information Society*, to President Carter in the Cabinet Room over ten years ago, and discussed our recommendations for federal action with him, he assured me of his administration's concern and that he would take prompt executive action. He asked me to have prepared a summarized version of our 654-page report so he could personally distribute it to each of his cabinet officers at its next meeting. It would be required reading for immediate action, he assured me. The White House did set up a task force and labored for two years before finally sending draft legislation to Congress, where it stimulated some hearings and much discussion, but no comprehensive action at the time.

Finally in the fall of 1986, President Reagan signed the Electronic Communications Privacy Act, expanding the scope of telecommunications covered under the protection of the 1968 federal wiretapping laws. As we had recommended, this act now gives protection to electronic mail, cellular telephones, pagers, and electronic data transmission, making private interception of these types of communication illegal. In addition, the law mandates that government agencies obtain court order approval before intercepting transmissions. As a result, the only types of communication exempted from coverage under the new provisions of the law are ham radio broadcasts, mobile and airline radios, paging devices using a tone but no message, radio portions of cordless phone calls, and other such types of radio transmission generally and readily accessible to the public at large.

Another new law, the Computer Fraud and Abuse Act, "makes it a crime to access a computer system from across state lines for fraudulent purpose." It sets up provisions to punish hackers who sell entry passwords belonging to other individuals and corporations.

These pieces of legislation, especially the Electronic Communications Privacy Act of 1986, have gone a long way toward enacting some of the recommendations contained in our report. Essentially they rectify loopholes in the 1968 wiretap legislation. They center on the fact that most data communication today involves machines rather than human-to-human conversations. These types of communication, including non-wire microwave, satellite, and optical transfers, are now protected.

One of the public-sector areas that concerned us, and which we asked Congress to consider, involved the Social Security Administration (SSA). SSA maintains files containing highly confidential information—records of income, assets and expenditures, institutional commitments, and medical conditions. Such data could be very useful to persons outside of government such as employees of insurance companies and banks as well as to persons with less than wholesome motives, and therefore it should be kept under secured conditions. Unfortunately, a test break-in at the time of our investigations was convincing evidence that the confidential data was not secure and could readily be accessed, without authorization.

In the private sector, for decades some organizations in this country have made part of their business operations obtaining, without authorization, confidential data from the files of hospitals, doctors, the Internal Revenue Service, and even the Federal Bureau of Investigation. The data thus obtained is then sold to some employers, insurance companies, and law firms. Various laws are not always adequate to cover this kind of improper activity, because they were designed to deal with theft of tangible property, not the theft of information about people.

The use of credit cards is the thread that weaves through the operations of business organizations and the lives of individuals, linking together what people read, where they travel, and with whom they associate. Records of credit card transactions are a rich source of information about the movements, purchases, associations, and life-styles of the cardholders. Not only do governmental authorities have access to these records, but so do nongovernmental investigators and resourceful competitors.

When a police officer was shot and killed outside a prominent New York restaurant and no witnesses came forward, police consulted American Express. In less than half a day the police were supplied with a list of twenty persons who had dined in the restaurant that night and had paid for their meals with credit cards. With the cooperation of these twenty diners, police were able to identify and apprehend the murderer. American Express has since amended its internal processes to supply such information only pursuant to a subpoena.

As reported by journalists Carl Bernstein and Bob Woodward in their book *All the President's Men* (1974), they used a similar approach in building their case against Donald Segretti during Watergate. They contacted an employee of a credit card company who provided them with information that Segretti had "crisscrossed the country more than ten times during the last half of 1971, according to his credit records, usually staying in a city for no longer than a night or two. . . . Many of the cities were in key political states for the 1972 presidential campaign, mostly primary states. In New Hampshire, Florida, Illinois, and particularly, California, Segretti had moved from city to city, leaving his trail in territories where the Democratic primaries would be fought hardest."

The ease with which unauthorized people obtain access to credit bureaus' computerized data banks was demonstrated by a data-theft ring based in Southern California. It had devised a scheme for providing good credit histories for people with poor credit ratings by using other people's credit profiles. This was accomplished by mixing up the confidential financial information in the data banks of the credit bureau.

Traditional Laws

Only a limited portion of computer crime can be successfully prosecuted under traditional, non-computer-specific law. State arson statutes may prove effective in prosecuting acts where a computer has been damaged by fire, either in an attempt to directly sabotage the computer or to eliminate evidence of other criminal activity.

When an individual enters a computer facility in an unlawful manner or for an unlawful purpose such as to damage the computer, steal software, or steal computer time, it is possible that a state's burglary statute may apply. However, if an individual attempts to gain access to the computer's software data in order to steal information or accesses the computer via remote terminals or secret telephone codes, attempted prosecution under traditional burglary statutes might be futile.

Larceny statutes prohibit the taking and carrying away of another's personal property without his consent and with the intention of permanently depriving him of it. These statutes clearly apply to situations where the object of the theft is transportable hardware such as minicomputers, magnetic tape or disks, or computer programs. But not all larceny statutes would cover the common situation where intangible software is simply copied and not physically carried away.

Embezzlement, defined as the unlawful appropriation of another's property by a person in a position of trust, is applicable to many computer crimes. A problem occurs when the clever computer embezzler creates no paper records of his illicit transaction, thereby avoiding detection. Also, certain states have been slow to follow the trend, and still do not consider intangible software programs to be property.

Impersonation of a legitimate systems user may be actionable under a forgery statute. In some jurisdictions with narrowly drawn statutory language, it may be necessary to prove that the misused entry codes can be transferred into written or printed form.

Criminal (malicious) mischief statutes prohibit the willful destruction of another's property. This offense requires an actual human action which is observable to a bystander, resulting in tangible damage to property. Such statutes adequately address hardware damage, but may be inapplicable to software damage, again because certain jurisdictions fail to consider software as "property." Even if a jurisdiction does consider software property, an absence of observable damage may forestall legal action under this category of legislation.

The offense of theft of services or labor under false pretenses requires that a perpetrator knowingly make a false representation to a victim with the intention of obtaining another's property. There must be injury to the victim resulting from reliance upon the false representation. Several states have also passed specific theft-of-credit-card statutes. As with other traditional theft statutes, problems may arise if the object of the theft is intangible property.

Interference-with-use or anti-tampering statutes prohibit unauthorized use of or interference with the property of another which results in a loss to the property owner. This may be an effective area of law to apply to a computer criminal who accesses a system from a remote location.

Even if your state is one of the few which has not yet enacted a comprehensive computer crime law, it is vital that you pursue any and all options available under traditional law if you are the victim of a computer criminal. A clear message must be sent to all present and potential computer criminals that such actions will no longer be tolerated and covered up, but will be prosecuted to the fullest extent possible under the law.

Computer Law

The Counterfeit Access Device and Computer Fraud and Abuse Act of 1984 prohibits fraudulent activity directed against certain computer systems. The limited provisions of the act declare that it is a felony, punishable by a fine of $10,000 and ten years imprisonment, to improperly access a computer to gain classified information. It is also a misdemeanor, punishable by a $5,000 fine and one year imprisonment, to improperly access and obtain information from the computer systems of a financial institution or a credit-reporting agency. To improperly access a computer operated for or on behalf of the U.S. government and to use, modify, destroy, or disclose information in, or prevent authorized use of the computer is also a misdemeanor.

As described earlier, the Electronic Communications Privacy Act of 1986 protects electronic mail, cellular telephones, pagers, and electronic data transmission. The Computer Fraud and Abuse Act of 1986 makes it a crime to access a computer across state lines for fraudulent purposes and provides for punishment to "hackers" who sell entry passwords belonging to others.

Under the Computer Software Act of 1980, the definition of a computer program was added to the Copyright Act of 1976, stating that such are to "be regarded as an extension of copyrightable subject matter Congress had already intended to protect."

To satisfy the statutory requirements for protection, a computer program must be original in its expression (created by the author, not copied) and must be fixed in a tangible medium of expression from which it can be perceived for more than a period of time. The media for a computer program may be printed form, punched cards, magnetic tape, silicon chips, or other suitable formats.

Once a program is copyrighted, the owner of the copyright has the exclusive rights to authorize the reproduction and distribution of copies of the copyrighted work, and to prepare derivative works based on the copyrighted work.

State Law

Computer-crime legislation is perhaps the most rapidly developing area of state legislation. In 1978, Florida became the first state to enact a computer crime law. Since that time, forty-six states have enacted such laws.

Computer crime statutes commonly serve two functions. First, they define computer data and software as property. This makes them subject to prosecution under theft, larceny, fraud, embezzlement, and other related traditional statutes. Alaska, Massachusetts, and Ohio have enacted this type of statute.

Second, they make the unauthorized access, use, modification, alteration, or obstruction of a computer system, computer program, or computer resources a crime. This is the more popular and comprehensive procedure.

California's statute contains typical language stating that it is a crime "to intentionally access . . . any computer system or computer network for the purpose of devising or executing any scheme or artifice; to defraud or extort or obtain money, property or services with false or fraudulent intent, representations, or promises; or to maliciously access, alter, delete, damage, or destroy, any computer system, computer network, computer program, or computer data."

Alabama, Colorado, Florida, Illinois, Missouri, Montana, and Wyoming statutes exercise both functions, prohibiting improper computer access and activity, and defining computer programs and data to be property.

There has been a recent trend toward incorporating computer crime legislation into the general provisions of state penal codes. In Virginia, for example, computer time and services have been defined as "property" that may be the object of larceny or embezzlement. Massachusetts and Ohio have also expanded their definitions of property to include electronically processed or stored data. In Alaska, deception of a machine, including a computer, is now a prosecutable offense.

Conclusion

Computers and the rapidly changing technology have both simplified and complicated men's lives. Although computer technology has added incredible speed and convenience to many aspects of modern life, it has also unlocked a Pandora's box for possible abuse.

Errors within a data base, whether intentional or not, must be minimized. Employees should be trained and performance monitored to avoid human error. The problem of intentional tampering is much more complicated.

The computer age introduced a new breed of intelligent, educated, white-collar criminal with an almost limitless capacity for harm. It is vital that laws keep pace with advancing technology. Although some laws in the last few years have been enacted, in general laws throughout the nation have not yet fully responded to the needs for protection. The use of appropriate internal controls in conjunction with adequate security, and a well-thought-out legal system are imperative if individual, corporate, and national privacy are to be protected.

6

Your Government Wants to Know

The deterioration of every government begins almost always by the decay of the principles on which it was founded.

—*Baron de Montesquieu*

All our freedoms are a single bundle, all must be secure if any is to be preserved.

—*Dwight David Eisenhower*

The United States government's thirst for information is not to be quenched. Year after year it grows. Many federal agencies have become omnivorous data-collectors, not always sufficiently concerned with protecting that data from abuse.

At the hub of the problem is the explosive growth in electronic data-processing technology. While the federal government may lag behind industry in some areas of management effectiveness, it does not lag in the collection of personal, sensitive information for its data banks. In 1962, there were 1,030 central processing units in federal agencies. By 1972, there were 6,731. By 1982, there were 18,747, an eighteen-fold increase in the number of computers operated by the federal government in that twenty-year period. Between 1983 and 1985, the number jumped to over 100,000. The federal government now has 27,000 mainframe computers, over 100,000 microcomputers, and over 170,000 mainframe computer terminals. This is the largest inventory of computers of any single organization in the world.

But this rate of growth will pale in comparison to the changes that lie ahead. Office of Management and Budget officials estimate that the number of personal computers with data-processing capabilities will grow to as many as one million by 1990, reflecting the decentralizing trends in computer and communications technologies. Incident to this proliferation is the potential for substantially increased abuse of the data contained in those computers. This chapter identifies some of the most intrusive government agencies and their practices, and outlines what you can do to protect your personal information from being abused.

At last count, in 1982, there were 3,530 million personal files on people in all federal agencies, or an average of 15 files for every man, woman, and child in America. Three-quarters of this data is held by five departments: Health and Human Services, Treasury, Education, Defense, and Commerce. During the three-year period covering fiscal years 1983 to 1985, the Department of Health and Human Services increased its spending on information technology by 23%; the Department of Energy increased by 33%; the Department of Defense by 41% percent; and the Justice Department (principally the FBI) by 65%.

Most Americans do not know the federal files they are in or what information about them has been gathered and can be tapped in a matter of minutes. Obviously, if you are a taxpayer, you are on file with the Internal Revenue Service; if you were in the military, you are on file with the Veterans Administration; if you ever applied for a passport, you have a record in the State Department; and just about everyone is on file with the Social Security Administration. Other records, however, are less obvious. For example:

- If you are an executive in a company that has military contracts, you are probably on file with the Defense Intelligence Agency.
- If your child ever applied for a student loan, you are probably on file with the Department of Education.
- If you were involved in a banking transaction exceeding $10,000, the Treasury Department has you on file.
- If you are a corporate officer, the Securities and Exchange Commission has a business profile on you.
- If a teenager in your family ever faced a drug or similar charge, the details are probably on file with the Justice Department.
- If you made a political contribution of $100 or more, a record on you is kept with the Clerk of Congress or Federal Election Commission.

The list goes on and on. In most cases, the purpose for collecting each individual record is appropriate and innocent enough. But put together, the total information available is uncomfortably complete and getting more extensive. For example, the Internal Revenue Service is using bigger computers, more state records, and a greater number of outside information sources in an attempt to stop tax fraud. And what happens if the information collected by government agencies gets into the wrong hands? Information is power. Personal information about you in the hands of governmental authorities can be abused. You should know who has what information, the use they make of it, and what you can do to protect yourself. As it stands, we have little assurance that someone won't misuse this information. For our own protection, each of us must be vigilant.

Small Worry or Major Concern?

According to an old Swedish proverb, worry often gives a small thing a big shadow. Are the dangers of abusive government merely imagined? I think not. A quarter century ago, U.S. Supreme Court Justice Potter Stewart wrote about the Fourth Amendment and the personal rights it secures to try to help secure against abusive government. Similarly, Justice Louis D. Brandeis wrote, "The makers of your Constitution sought to protect Americans. . . . They conferred, as against the government, the right to be let alone. . . . To protect that right, every unjustifiable intrusion by the government upon the privacy of individual, whatever the means employed, must be deemed a violation of the Fourth Amendment. . . ." A report issued by the National Bureau of Standards concluded that: "The Watergate disclosures of how top officials of the federal executive branch abused Internal Revenue Service records, conducted mail covers and openings, used illegal wiretapping and bugging, spied on political critics and dissident groups, and resorted to burglaries and break-ins came as a shock to the American public. All the 'what if' warnings of civil libertarians about possible misuse of government powers suddenly became real rather than hypothetical situations."

Apart from sinister motives, there is a constant risk of human error as record keeping and surveillance activities continue to mushroom. In Illinois, federal agents on the trail of narcotics dealers violently raided the home of an innocent family only to learn that the address in the police files was wrong.

The National Security Agency's (NSA) capability for intercepting international telegram and Telex messages of United States citizens is so sophisticated that it is ripping open legal protections of individual privacy. In 1982, a Federal Appeals Court ruled that the National Security Agency may listen in on conversations between U.S. citizens and people overseas, even when there is no reason to suspect the American citizen of being a foreign agent. John Shattuck, the ACLU attorney who appealed the case, wrote, "It is difficult to imagine a more sweeping judicial approval of governmental action in violation of constitutional rights than the decision of the panel in this case." A report by the Senate Select Committee on Intelligence concluded, "The National Security Agency's potential to violate the privacy of American citizens is unmatched by any other intelligence agency."

At the same time the National Security Agency is taking steps to try to protect government's telephone messages. In 1985, it initiated a five-year program to encode information sent on the nation's telephone and data networks by federal agencies and contractors. While the main threat of messages being intercepted comes from the Soviet Union, there is concern about tampering by domestic industrial spies or computer hackers as well. Unauthorized surveillance has become more of a problem since most messages are transmitted by satellites or microwave and as such are much more susceptible to being monitored.

According to the National Security Agency, the Soviets are now able to eavesdrop on the nation's telephone and data networks from facilities on ships and in Washington, Long Island, San Francisco, and Cuba. Such surveillance and the use of the information that is obtained can have unusual effects. For example, several years ago it was speculated within the National Security Council that the Soviets used information obtained by eavesdropping on American grain dealers to their advantage in purchasing grain from us.

The government has begun installing computers that keep detailed records of telephone calls made by federal employees. The new computers record local and long distance calls, detailing the date of the call, length of the call, the call's origin, and the call's destination. The government says the system is designed to enable managers to provide cheaper and more efficient telephone service, but Frank Carr, Chief of Communications for the General Services Administration, says it raises questions about employee privacy rights. In addition, there are few laws that protect government employees in this situation. Carr said he is not aware of any agency that has rules governing the new technology's use, and there is no federal law that restricts the use of any of this information. However, once the data becomes a system of records and is identified to a specific individual, that individual is then protected by the Privacy Act.

In 1986 the President's Council on Integrity and Efficiency collected detailed information from historical records about personal long-distance phone calls of federal employees to reduce the number of improper telephone calls. This information became available upon the installation of new computerized telephone switching equipment. Congresspersons Don Edwards and Patricia Schroeder are concerned that sufficient controls must be designed to ensure that this system not be used "to discourage whistle blowers, to stifle dissent, to limit news media access to information or for other political purposes."

The Reagan administration has put off its plan to make census information available to other government agencies. Presently, the Census Bureau is required by law to keep confidential the data it collects. The tabled plan would have required the bureau to share the data it collects with other agencies.

As recently as three decades ago, a person's daily activities—financial and personal—were generally beyond the government's reach, except when crimes were involved. Today, records are, as a matter of course, made available to the government whether such disclosure is required or not. Except for some limited restrictions provided by the Financial Privacy Act of 1978, a record keeper may disclose information about an individual to the government voluntarily without the individual being able to intervene.

At a Senate Judiciary Subcommittee hearing some time ago, the then Senator Charles Mathias, Jr., R-MD, argued that "under present law, the privacy of Americans may turn on technical questions—whether or not the communication is carried by wire, whether it is analog or digital form—that are simply irrelevant to the legitimate expectations" of privacy people have expected when using communications networks.

The Most Intrusive Government Agencies

Your securities being held by your stockbroker and the records of your stock transactions are not inviolate information. A Securities and Exchange Commission official can visit your stockbroker's office and examine your account without a summons of any kind. The SEC is given authority under the 1934 Securities Exchange Act to inspect stockbrokers' records. It has a routine inspection function as well as responsibility to investigate cases of wrongdoing. Such records are also obtained through the mail, according to Rick Norell of the SEC's enforcement division. If they can't be obtained that way, he says, "we can just walk in." There is very little that the SEC cannot obtain.

The technical issues can lead to difficult legal interpretations. For example, the Electronic Communications Privacy Act of 1986 set up varying levels of protection for "electronic" versus "oral" or "wire" transmissions. A telephone could potentially involve a combination of all three of these methods. Trying to apply privacy protections here through a series of varying levels of security can be very confusing for lawyers and judges as well as for typical citizens.

Social security files containing confidential information on millions of Americans are also uncomfortably penetrable. Some years ago, investigators employed by the General Accounting Office, testing the system, slipped out of the Social Security System's national computer center in Baltimore with a cart of tapes containing the names and addresses of 1.14 million beneficiaries. Despite the fact that the Social Security Administration had spent a half million dollars on a new security system, the GAO team found thousands of computer cards stacked in the hallways and secretly moved them out through security stations and emergency exits. They found that unauthorized personnel had access to the computer room and tape storage area, and that social security and Medicare magnetic tapes and disk packs could be removed without proper authorization. Although the report describing this incident was just one in a series of reports issued by GAO over the past decade, GAO officials today believe the physical security has improved. As far as electronic access is concerned, however, the safeguards are less clear.

Protect yourself by not giving out your social security number unless it is absolutely required. Federal law provides that government benefits may not be denied an individual for refusal to provide a social security number unless, prior to 1975, there was a law or regulation authorizing such a demand. In any case, state, local, and federal agencies must notify an individual of the authority that allows them to collect the social security number and what uses will be made of it. The Tax Reform Act of 1976 has removed state welfare, tax, and motor vehicle agencies from this restriction. The law now provides criminal penalties for disclosing or using a person's social security number contrary to federal laws.

Do you know who is reading your mail? Even though current operational data is not available, it is known that the Central Intelligence Agency had been found guilty of opening United States citizens' mail to and from the Soviet Union as part of a domestic surveillance program. Between 1953 and 1973, the CIA opened around 215,000 letters and distributed them to other agencies. The CIA also noted the names of every person mentioned in the correspondence (around 1.5 million people) and stored the names in computers. Using a special chemical to decipher the writing inside, it is understood they were also able to read the mail without opening the envelope.

Although the Postal Service has said that it no longer allows the CIA to intercept mail, it is known that FBI agents may still get warrants to do so. Court orders are issued for this purpose about two hundred times a year.

It is less well known that the Customs Service had been opening international mail that it believed might contain contraband. Mail openings are not unconstitutional as long as federal laws and regulations are followed. But according to postal officials, the customs practices were "highly irregular," and customs officials allegedly read mail without a search warrant, had delayed mail for up to ninety days, and had turned over intercepted mail to military investigators.

Recently the Department of Agriculture asked for "authority to open and detain" first-class mail to check for Mediterranean fruit flies. USDA officials want to inspect packages arriving in California from Hawaii and Puerto Rico for the presence of pests and have petitioned Congress for permission to make the checks without warrants.

In 1976, the Supreme Court ruled that opening international mail does not violate the Fourth Amendment provided the Customs Service agent has "reasonable cause" to believe that the envelopes contain dutiable goods or contraband. Although there is no right to read the mail opened, to believe that this does not go on would be naive. *Privacy Journal* publisher Robert Ellis Smith asserts that evidence exists that customs officers regularly read mail as part of their investigative duties, even though no warrant has been obtained.

If you suspect your mail has been opened, contact the postmaster general and state attorney general. It is a crime for anyone, without authority, to open or destroy any mail not directed to him. A search warrant must be obtained before domestic, first-class mail may be opened, and a court order is required before mail suspected of violations may be detained.

Internal Revenue Service

Few, if any, government agencies have more potential for abusing individual financial privacy than the Internal Revenue Service. Here is what perceptive journalist James B. Stewart of the *Wall Street Journal* had to say after going through an IRS audit of his 1983 tax return. ". . . I felt my privacy was in shreds. My auditor knows more about my life during that year, I suppose, than anyone else on earth—whom I had dinner with, whom I made phone calls to, where I traveled, how I spent my money and where my deposits came from. I was amazed at the extent to which explanations of financial records reveal virtually every aspect of one's life."

Since 1910 taxpayer returns were "public records," and both the White House and Treasury Department had broad discretion in making them available to other persons. After the Nixon administration had allegedly used tax returns to harass its political opponents, however, Congress resolved to place certain restrictions on the use of IRS records by enacting the Tax Reform Act of 1976. That act established the principle that "returns and return information shall be confidential." In passing this legislation, Congress took on direct responsibility for determining permissible disclosures. Thus the revised Section 6103 of the IRS code establishes confidentiality unless disclosure is specifically authorized by statute. The act also prohibits "redisclosure," so that government agencies that obtain tax information are prohibited from transmitting it elsewhere.

From 1976, the principle of confidentiality has gradually eroded, however. The steady addition of exemptions to the rule prompted the Senate Subcommiteee on Oversight of Government Management to hold hearings on the question in June 1984. While the then IRS Commissioner Roscoe L. Egger insisted that this is still "in reality a nondisclosure statute that generally prohibits the release of taxpayer information," it was noted that there are at least twenty-nine different exceptions to the rule. The major programs involve the release of millions of taxpayer records for a variety of investigative and enforcement activities. The importance of this information has expanded the role of our tax-collecting authorities. As former IRS Commissioner Donald C. Alexander remarked at that same hearing, "The tax system is carrying too much baggage. It shouldn't carry any more. IRS should not be the nation's tax collector, as well as the nation's all-purpose debt collector."

Tax authorities traditionally have sought to increase their intrusiveness into peoples' lives. The Carter administration scrapped plans for an $850 million, 8,300-terminal, nationwide computer network the IRS wanted, due in large part to concerns about personal privacy and the power this could give to a single government agency. This operation, dubbed Tax Administration System (TAS), would have updated our entire tax-processing system. The IRS would have been able to take advantage of "real time" data handling, updating records at the moment that transactions occurred. It would have involved the latest in computer technology, and would have given us a much more efficient and economical service. But it also would have given thousands of IRS employees instant access to the tax records of more than 103 million individual and corporate taxpayers. Nevertheless, in recent years, the IRS has installed extensive computer systems throughout its network.

"What we fail to realize," noted the director of the National Bureau of Standards, "is that we have little skill and experience in even asking the appropriate questions to enable an adequate technology assessment of a computerized record-keeping network that would handle information of such national significance."

It should be noted that the IRS has continued to develop and refine a system called the Taxpayer Compliance Measurement Program (TCMP). This is a computer-assisted process to help IRS predict the behavior of every American taxpayer. Essentially this is a predictive model based on a randomly selected sample of taxpayers. The system provides an estimate of the sort of citizens likely to try to cheat the government, and allows IRS to concentrate its investigative resources on this target group.

According to the General Accounting Office, the IRS has already opened the door to widespread abuse of confidential federal income tax records. In a lengthy report, the GAO criticized the IRS for its inadequate control over computer operations (programmers could easily run a program without authorization or make an unauthorized program change with little or no fear of discovery), its hardware shortcomings (microfilm equipment was unable to produce a transcript for one taxpayer, but included unnecessary data on many other taxpayers), and its failure to enforce strict screening procedures for employees.

Unfortunately, such abuse and carelessness ripples far beyond the IRS. More often than not, the right-hand-not-knowing-what-the-left-hand-is-doing syndrome does not seem to hold true here. When it comes to exchanging information about people under investigation, according to one official, "We work for the same uncle; we're like one big family."

At the present time, the IRS shares data with many other government bodies, including federal agencies and state and local tax units. The IRS says it has strict rules when handing out records, but who is to say how closely they are being enforced and if those rules are effective.

The IRS has supplied information from one year's tax returns on nearly 63 million people to tax departments of various states. Several thousand returns in a six-month period alone were requested by federal agencies, although not every one of them was necessarily turned over. These agencies include the Justice Department, the Social Security Administration, the Securities and Exchange Commission, and the Department of Health and Human Services.

Currently, the IRS is allowed to disclose to the Department of Education the names and addresses of taxpayers who have defaulted on student loans; they can disclose to the National Institute for Occupational Safety and Health the identities of those persons who may have been exposed to occupational health hazards. It is authorized to engage in a number of nontax activities such as offsetting the tax refunds of persons who are delinquent in making child-support payments and forwarding letters on behalf of other government agencies. These disclosures are permitted through Section 6103 of the Internal Revenue Code, revised in 1976, which tries to specify and limit the number of authorized disclosures of tax information.

The recent amendments to the Omnibus Budget Reconciliation Act of 1984, which established the first statutory protections for computer matching, are encouraging. Beneficiaries of certain government programs must now be notified that IRS and social security data may be used to disqualify them for benefits. Any adverse determination resulting from a computer match may not be used to reduce or terminate benefits without independent verification of the information received. This provision is designed to protect beneficiaries who might have been penalized because of computer error or reporting discrepancies. If you receive an adverse determination concerning a government program, ask what grounds were used in making that decision. If it was based on government records, demand a copy of the records involved and challenge any inaccuracies or misrepresentations that you find.

Our voluntary income tax system is a rare commodity. Only a limited number of nations in the world have such a system. The Internal Revenue Service is primarily responsible for the collection of taxes. Any activity in which the IRS might participate should be thoughtfully evaluated by government authorities to assure that taxpayers are not discouraged from disclosing all the information on a tax return so that the taxes due are properly computed. Full disclosure might be threatened by taxpayers' fears that some of the information they provide may be submitted to another agency for another purpose. For most taxpayers, fair information practice could be instituted if the IRS were required to inform taxpayers when it discloses individually identifiable data to another agency, even if such notice were to be in the aggregate by widespread public notice. In the most sensitive areas, where appropriate, even consent of the taxpayer might be obtained. Exceptions, if necessary, could be made for carefully monitored categories such as criminal prosecution, census taking, or the extraction of key data by state tax agencies.

Third-Party Reactions to IRS Probes

Some third parties have resisted IRS attempts to gain new information sources. An IRS plan to use marketing lists prepared by Donnelley Marketing Service, R. L. Polk, and Metromail failed when the companies refused to make their lists available on the grounds that it would be improper. The IRS wanted to compare names of high-income earners to taxpayers lists to look for cheats. But the marketing companies said their data was only reliable on an aggregate, not individual, basis, and that IRS use might impinge on people's privacy. How long this attitude will hold is open to question.

Alexander Hoffman, Chairman of the Direct Marketing Association, explained the dangers: "The more we analyze the possible consequences of the IRS' use of mailing lists, the more convinced we become of the wisdom of not using data for a purpose different from that for which it was collected, or from that for which the person from whom it was collected expects it to be used. . . . Private sector mailing lists, no matter from which sources they are compiled, are used for marketing purposes, and in no case are used to discover specific data about a specific person."

In practice, IRS use of mailing lists is not always as benign as it should be. The IRS advertised in business publications for "life-style" demographic mailing lists. One respondent offered data on 35 million families with details including sex and age of all members of the household, recent mail purchases and amounts, religion, ethnic group, telephone number, approximate income, length of residence and dwelling size, children's birthdays, census tract, and postal carrier. The IRS compared this data with tax returns to see that people are paying taxes commensurate with their life-styles.

Fair information practice requires that taxpayers be informed about any procedure using their personal data, with appropriate exception for established and approved, fully accountable law enforcement needs. As in so many other areas, achieving the goal of balancing the needs of the individual for personal information protection against the relevant needs of society's institutions for effective management must be constantly sought in the taxing function of government by all branches.

Government Assistance Programs

About 39 million of the 83.6 million households in the United States contain one or more participants in government assistance programs. Federal outlays for these benefits, totaling $365 billion for FY 1986, are estimated to remain at about 43% to 44% of total federal expenditures. At the latest count, there were 72 needs- or insurance-based programs in existence.

In March 1985, the General Accounting Office published a report entitled *Eligibility Verification and Privacy in Federal Benefit Programs: A Delicate*

Balance which exposed the complexity of the verification process. To ensure proper eligibility decisions, vast amounts of accurate, complete, and current information must be collected and stored. This naturally entails individuals having to reveal information about themselves that they may feel is private. Hence the GAO report defined the issue as follows: "An appropriate amount of relevant data, checked in the most effective and efficient manner, without unduly intruding into client privacy—that is the goal the eligibility verification process should seek." It is also the goal that we are a long way from attaining.

Between the federal government and the states, the welfare system involves a complex set of eligibility criteria for determining who can collect and how much they are entitled to receive. Applying these criteria requires a constant review of personal and confidential data. The welfare system, by its very nature and function, is intrusive. It was not always so.

At the end of the eighteenth century, welfare was a cash subsidy for farm laborers in England whose income had sunk so low that everyone knew they needed help. During the Industrial Revolution, an army of dispossessed and unemployable citizens was added to those few thousand impoverished farm laborers. Relief was granted through the odious institution called the workhouse, so shameful and humiliating that one would do anything short of starving to avoid it. The workhouse/poorhouse concept was exported to America. Needless to say, there was little welfare fraud in those days.

During the Depression of the 1930s, unemployment was commonplace, and the federal government took over major welfare responsibilities. The stigma of accepting aid that carried force in small towns, that of being denigrated by one's neighbors, mattered less in large urban centers. Also, the concept of welfare changed. Instead of the limited objective of furnishing the absolute minimum of food, shelter, and clothing requirements, modern welfare tried to help people overcome the conditions that made them poor. This goal increased the level of intrusiveness.

Present laws provide no clear and consistent policies on personal record-keeping in federally assisted welfare programs. Individual laws relate to specific programs, with the result that program administrators often encounter inconsistent, and sometimes incompatible, regulations governing record keeping. Regulations concerning this vast and complex network are ambiguous. Simplification along with broadly and generally applicable standards are desperately needed.

In the area of student financial aid, there are regulations which may be compatible with other government programs, but are incompatible with an individual's expectations of confidentiality. For example, an Illinois professional applied to a government agency for a nursing school loan, and, as part of the application, was required to supply a parents' financial statement. Forty-six years of age and married for almost two decades, she justifiably believed that her parents' financial situation was irrelevant to her application. In a letter to the financial director of the program, the applicant wrote, "I certainly will disclose all the information about my financial situation that should enable you to make a decision in my case. I protest and refuse to submit my parents' financial statement. It would be a distinct invasion of my parents' privacy and totally irrelevant to the matter at hand." The requirement of financial statements from the applicant's parents was finally waived.

Several years ago, the New York State Health Department undertook a federally financed study on the effects of abortion covering 48,000 women. Former New York State Senator Karen S. Burstein and Assemblyman Mark Siegel asked the state's Health Commission to halt work on the study until the women gave their consent. They described the study as a "massive invasion of privacy," and produced a Health Department progress report containing a "sample output" which included the names of twenty-eight women who had had abortions and were subsequently married. The report had been filed with the National Institute of Health, which was financing the study, and was distributed "casually, almost randomly." The public outcry at the time forced the department to cease the practice. New York has now passed legislation controlling state and local governments' use of information on pregnancy termination.

Computer Matching

Computer matching refers to the comparison of different lists or files of individuals to discover duplication, fraud, cheating, or other abuse in any program. Comparisons can be made using any personal identifier, including names, social security numbers, and addresses.

Early in the matching program in 1977, the then Secretary of Health, Education and Welfare announced with much publicity the beginning of "Project Match." The program was aimed at identifying those government employees who were illegally receiving benefits from the HEW's Aid to Families with Dependent Children (AFDC) program. It involved the comparison of computer tapes of welfare roles and federal payroll files in the Washington, D.C., area. This was the pilot project for the eventual nationwide match of five million employee records with welfare roles in 26 states. Subsequently, federal agencies initiated 126 benefit-related matches, 38 of which were still in effect by May 1984. State agencies as of October 1982 had initiated more than 1,200 matching projects, most of them on a recurring basis.

Most matching has been done after clients receive benefits. However, between 1982 and 1984 the trend toward front-end matching—that is, matching before benefits are granted—doubled, according to the President's Council on Integrity and Efficiency. The Income and Eligibility Verification Process section of the Deficit Reduction Act of 1984 made front-end matching mandatory for all states as of 1 October 1987; by 1 October 1988 all states were required to have wage-reporting data bases.

Examples of federal government matches include: federal personnel records with files of Veterans Administration hospital employees; 1982 IRS records of taxpayers addresses with lists of individuals born in 1963 supplied by the Selective Service System to locate suspected violators of the draft registration law; and Labor Department files of persons entitled to receive black lung benefits with Health and Human Services Department records of Medicare billings to probe medical fraud. About to be added is the comparison of names of retired employees drawing pensions with lists of government employees getting workers compensation for on-the-job injuries or occupational diseases; this is designed to catch double payments.

We have also seen a dramatic increase in the number of matching programs at the state and local levels. The city of New York has agreed to exchange tax information on individuals and businesses with the IRS. Computers will be used to cross-check tax returns filed with the federal government and the city in an effort to identify taxpayers who file with the IRS but fail to pay their city taxes. New York City Finance Commissioner Abraham Biderman says the program initiated in 1987, which is the first of its kind in the nation, may bring in "tens of millions" of dollars in additional revenue for the city.

Not all the "hits" that computers identify are wrongdoers. Computer and human error must be taken into account. Back-up research and investigation must be undertaken before corrective action can be considered. The Illinois Public Aid Department estimates that half of the "hits" discovered when searching private and public employees' records for welfare cheats are bogus.

In Massachusetts, the Department of Public Welfare at first took action solely on the basis of the computer spin-off. It matched state welfare roles with Massachusetts bank accounts and automatically struck people from welfare whose bank accounts showed they were over the various eligibility limits. "Project Bank Match" quickly resulted in many complaints and some litigation, forcing the welfare department to initiate a fact-finder program. Currently the procedure requires sending a letter to those exposed by the match with a request for an explanation. Tom Devouton, Director of Special Projects at the Massachusetts Department of Welfare, states that this practice brings Massachusetts into line with other states.

Civil libertarians claim that any matching is a *prima facie* violation of the Fourth Amendment, which protects against unreasonable searches and seizures. The courts have prohibited "fishing expeditions" in people's houses on the chance that something might turn up. Similarly, some civil rights activists complain that the technique of matching unrelated computer tapes is intentionally designed as a general search and is not based on any pre-existing evidence to direct suspicion of wrongdoing.

Agencies argue that if people have done nothing wrong they have nothing to fear. But, as Senator William Cohen remarked at a Senate hearing in August 1986, the attitude seems to be that privacy is only invaded when "we send people in trench coats and large-brimmed hats inquiring down the street about your finances." Whereas, he claims the unwarranted disclosure of the information itself is a threat to privacy, whether it be improper rummaging through your house, or running a computer tape. With specific reference to computer matching, Senator Cohen argues that "unless properly conducted and controlled, it can pose serious threats to the privacy and due process rights of individuals whose records are matched. . . . In matching programs, individuals can have crucial government benefits reduced or terminated solely on the basis of unverified information produced by a computer match—information that can be out of date, misleading, or just plain wrong. Citizens can be— and have been in the past—placed in the difficult position of having to defend themselves against information that has never even been reviewed by a human being for its accuracy" (*Congressional Record*, S11746, 8/14/86).

The federal Privacy Act stipulates that agencies shall not disclose personal information contained in a system of records without the "prior consent of the individual to whom the record pertains." But there is a wide exception: if the disclosure is a "routine use" for purposes "compatible with the purposes for which it was collected," the provision does not apply. The transfer of computer tapes from the source agency to the matching agency is considered a "routine use," and therefore individuals do not have to be informed.

Is such a use "compatible with the purposes for which it was collected"? Agencies have used some rather vague and expansive definitions of compatibility. For example, in 1980 the Office of Personnel Management (OPM) released some of its records to help the Veterans Administration check the accreditation of its hospital employees. OPM claimed that the disclosure constituted a "routine use" of its data because the agency believed "that an integral part of the reason that these records are maintained is to protect the legitimate interests of government, and therefore, such a disclosure is compatible with the purposes of maintaining these records."

The IRS believes it derives consent of the taxpayer to disclose your tax data to others with the statement contained on its "Instructions for Preparing Form 1040." The instructions state, "We may give the information to the Department of Justice and to other Federal agencies, as provided by law. We may also give it to the states, the District of Columbia, and U.S. commonwealths, or possessions to carry out their tax laws. And we may give it to foreign governments because of tax treaties they have with the United States."

Some individuals have experienced hardships as a result of matching without proper safeguards. A woman with cervical cancer had to quit nursing school and go on welfare. After months of treatment, her doctor said she could go back to work, and she found a job with a Health and Human Services agency.

She notified welfare twice that she had a job, but she kept receiving checks. One time, in order to pay for her medical treatment, she cashed one of the welfare checks. A computer match turned up her name and she was questioned by investigators. As a result of the interrogation, she left her job. Three months later, her name appeared in a newspaper as a welfare cheat. A court-appointed attorney advised her to plead guilty, which she was about to do when the judge asked her if she had notified the welfare agency about her taking a job. On finding out that she had twice notified the agency, the judge threw the case out of court.

In Massachusetts, as a result of "Project Bank Match," an elderly woman in a nursing home was taken off the Medicaid rolls after the match turned up a bigger balance in her bank account than permitted. What the computer did not know was that most of the money was being held in trust to pay the woman's funeral expenses and did not affect Medicaid eligibility.

The Illinois Labor Department used its hits wrongly to deny benefits to certain aliens who were not yet listed as legal residents by the Immigration and Naturalization Service. Since that time, Illinois has been able to claim actual yearly savings of $5 million to $6 million through its Project SAVE— Systematic Alien Verification for Entitlement. Governor Thompson, Commissioner of Immigration and Naturalization Service (INS) Alan C. Nelson, and then Attorney General William French Smith were so impressed with the project that the INS made the program available nationwide. SAVE allows federal, state, and local entitlement agencies to use an INS data base containing information on legal permanent resident aliens to determine the eligibility of applicants for benefits. Under the Immigration Reform and Control Act of 1986, all states were required to participate in SAVE as of 1 October 1988.

Spinning a reel of magnetic tape against its counterpart to identify wrong-doers and ineligibles is presented as a cost-effective way for government to operate an internal control mechanism. To protect due process and constitutional rights, however, this effort should also involve detailed and, where necessary, extensive follow-up efforts. As mentioned earlier, more and more agencies are turning to "front-end verification"—matching the data before any benefits are provided. This procedure avoids erroneous payments at the outset, and better preserves privacy and due process rights. But questions remain before front-end matching can be confidently proclaimed as the solution to government's problems in detecting fraud and abuse. As a March 1985 GAO report asked: "Is front-end matching more effective than the usual verification procedures? . . . Is front-end matching cost effective and cost beneficial? . . . Are the matched data readily available, accurate, complete, and current? . . . What eligibility factors should be matched? . . . Will front-end matching unduly delay eligible clients' receipt of initial benefits?" It gave no answers.

Computer matching operations were stimulated by a successful program in the medical field. In that project, 252 million Medicaid bills from 231,000 physicians and 44,000 pharmacists were run through the computer. If a patient visited the same doctor more than forty times a year or if a doctor reported more than one hysterectomy on the same patient, for example, the computer flagged the information as suspicious. As a result, about 10 percent of the doctors' bills and half of those submitted by pharmacists received further scrutiny.

Officials from the IRS said they recovered $1.8 billion in taxes in 1984 by expanding the electronic scanning of income tax returns and matching the results with dividend and interest statements from banks and brokers. Two technological advances helped the IRS to recover the money. One is the use of magnetic tape by nearly all dividend-reporting corporations, and the other is the introduction of optical scanners that read handwritten numbers on tax returns and translate them into computer-readable data on tape. According to IRS official Fred P. Williams, deputy assistant tax commissioner in charge of examining returns, the use of the new technology will "substantially increase the IRS's presence" in people's lives.

One form of computer matching has caused considerable concern, even though it was instituted to assure equal justice to all. Breaking a precedent started by Ronald Reagan and Edmund Brown when they were governors of California, Governor George Deukmejian approved the turnover of the names and addresses of men of draft age listed on the driver's license rolls. About 60,000 names were given to the Selective Service in California. Nationally, all states except for Kansas, Montana, and Hawaii now provide these lists to the Selective Service.

Matching programs are appropriate internal control techniques for assuring equitable and effective administration of programs required in a society that wrestles with the problems of providing increased economic opportunities for our deprived neighbors and large budget deficits. They can be, and in many instances now are, operated with adequate and fair privacy protections. Fairness depends on how matching is implemented.

For example, sending computer tapes of welfare rolls to employers to be matched against their payrolls is improper because some people attach a stigma to the need to receive welfare. Reversing the process, however, and arranging for employers to submit tapes of the gainfully employed workers to the welfare agencies in the area for matching does not unreasonably impose on the privacy rights of the entitlement recipients. Also, matching of welfare rolls against data in other government agencies' records is justified, if done with discretion. In all matching procedures, the individuals concerned should be notified that such matching will take place.

Access to Government Files

More than fourteen years ago, Congress passed the Privacy Act of 1974 giving citizens the right to see and correct all records held about them by the federal government. The law did not, however, establish a system to inform people of this right. As a result, few have taken advantage of the law to check their records. For example, the Social Security Administration is a huge organization involving more than 150 million Americans, yet only twenty-three people asked to see their records in 1986. This low level of interest is worrying some government officials. The White House Office of Management and Budget is responsible for overseeing the Privacy Act. Officials there say they want to make more people aware of its provisions by changing the way the government currently announces them. "Although we're clearly abiding by the letter of the law, we also want to support its spirit," said the OMB Deputy Director Joseph Wright, Jr. "That's why we are going to be looking at the publications the government puts out on its programs to make sure they provide better explanations of individual rights under the Privacy Act."

The General Accounting Office has also shown some concern that the public is not aware of its rights to see records. In a review of program applications, the GAO found that only two of more than fifty application forms stated in writing that citizens had the right to see their files. Representative Glenn English, D-OK, the chairman of the House Government Operations Information Subcommittee, proposed a bill which would create a small, permanent agency to "fight for individual privacy. . . . If the government does not advise the people of their rights, the rights will not be exercised." Spokesmen for both the IRS and the Social Security Administration said their agencies do not publicize citizens' rights to see files because the law does not specifically require them to do so.

As stated earlier, under the Federal Privacy Act of 1974, you have the right to examine information on file about you in any federal government agency, subject to specific exceptions mainly dealing with security interests. Make any such request as specific as you can, citing the Privacy Act of 1974 in your letter. If you are required to pay a fee for this service, it must be limited to the costs of search and duplication. If you are denied access, you can file a civil action against the agency. If you prevail in this suit, the court will assess reasonable litigation costs against the United States. You may also request the amendment of a record concerning yourself. Such a request must be promptly acknowledged in writing and, if the request is refused, the agency must inform you of the procedures for an administrative appeal.

If your request under the Privacy Act is unsuccessful, request the records under the Freedom of Information Act (FOIA). The procedure to be followed is essentially the same as for Privacy Act requests, but the exemptions from disclosure are somewhat different, so a FOIA request may be successful when a Privacy Act request was not.

How to Request Personal Records

If you think that a particular agency maintains records concerning you, write to the head of that agency or to the Privacy Act Officer. A sample request letter can be found at the end of this chapter. Agencies are required to inform you, at your request, whether they have files on you.

The *United States Government Manual* lists all federal agencies and describes their functions. In addition, it usually lists their local and regional office addresses and telephone numbers. The manual can be found in most libraries, and can be purchased for $20.00 by writing to the Superintendent of Documents, U.S. Government Printing Office, Washington, D.C. 20402. The *Congressional Directory* can also be of use since, like the manual, it lists the administrators of the various agencies. This too is available in most public libraries and can be purchased from the Government Printing Office for $15.00.

If you want to make a more thorough search to determine what records federal departments may have, you should consult the compilation of Privacy Act notices published annually in the *Federal Register*. This multivolume work contains descriptions of all federal records systems. It describes the kinds of data covered by the systems and lists the categories of individuals to whom the information pertains. It also includes the procedures that different agencies follow in helping individuals who request information about their records, and it specifies the agency official to whom you should write to find out whether you are the subject of a file. The *Federal Register* is usually available in large reference, law, and university libraries.

While it may be helpful to agency officials for you to specify a particular record system which you think contains information concerning you, it is not necesssary to provide this information. If you have a general idea of the record you want, don't hesitate to write the agency which you think maintains it.

You can make a request in writing, by telephone, or in person. One advantage to writing is that it enables you to document the dates and contents of the request and the agency's replies. This could be helpful in the event of future disputes. Be sure to keep copies of all correspondence concerning the request.

Your request should be addressed to the head of the agency which maintains the records you want or to the agency official specified in the *Federal Register*. Be sure to write "Privacy Act Request" on the bottom left-hand corner of the envelope. Along with your name and permanent address, you should always give as much information as possible about the record you are seeking. The more specific the inquiry, the faster you can expect a response.

Most agencies require some proof of identity before they will release records. Therefore, when making your request, it would be a good idea to provide some identifying data such as a copy of an official document containing your complete name and address. Remember, too, to sign your request since a signature provides a form of identification. You might also want to consider having your signature notarized. If you are seeking access to a record which has something to do with a government benefit, it would be helpful to include your social security number. Some agencies may request additional information, such as a document containing your signature and/or photograph, depending upon the nature and sensitivity of the material to be released.

Anyone who "knowingly and willfully" requests or receives access to a record about an individual "under false pretenses" is subject to criminal penalties. This means that a person can be prevented from deliberately attempting to obtain someone else's record.

All of the foregoing involves only records kept by the federal government. You are also on file with many state and municipal agencies. State records include births and deaths of all members of your family, all automobile registrations as well as licensed automobile drivers, and all recipients of state entitlement programs. Local records tell how much you paid for your house, what its current value is, whether you were ever in bankruptcy proceedings, or if you have a tax lien against you. Personal information on your boat, car, and gun permits are prime sources for private credit investigators.

Ten states have enacted Fair Information Practices acts which reflect the principles embodied in the federal Privacy Act of 1974: Arkansas, California, Connecticut, Indiana, Massachusetts, Minnesota, New York, Ohio, Utah, and Virginia. California's law, enacted in 1978, is similar to those in other states. It permits citizens the right to see and correct state files about themselves. State agencies may disclose personal information only in limited circumstances. The state university system and police are exempt. Unlike other states, California permits invasion-of-privacy lawsuits against a person who intentionally discloses personal information that he or she should have known came from a state or federal agency in violation of law. Four other states— Colorado, Illinois, Kentucky, and Texas—allow citizens access to records relating to them as well as the right to challenge information believed to be inaccurate.

All fifty states have enacted some type of open records legislation. If your state has not legislated express privacy legislation, contact your state's attorney and ask what information is available under your state's public records laws.

Corrective Action Clearly Called For

A number of states have passed Fair Information Practices acts which both limit the disclosure of personal data in state systems and allow people to see and correct their own files. As far as restrictions upon disclosure to federal agencies are concerned, however, confusion reigns.

The appetite of some administrators and many investigators for information causes them to collect any personal data they can, unless doing so is clearly unlawful. This focus on avoiding what is improper rather than concentrating on only what is necessary leads to privacy abuses. Basic legal and moral protections of citizens' privacy rights evolved before modern investigative agencies and their massive electronic record-keeping techniques appeared. Today's ability for large-scale intensive abuses was not envisioned when safeguards against government intrusion were established. As technology continues to increase its capacity for intrusion, and as we continue to expect more and more from government at all levels, constant vigilance of intrusive behavior by government administrators increasingly will have to become a way of life. We must become familiar with our rights, which have been described throughout this chapter, and take the initiative to enforce them.

Sample Request Letter

Agency Head or Privacy Act Officer
Title
Agency
Address of Agency
City, State, Zip

RE: Privacy Act Request

Dear _____:

Under the provisions of the Privacy Act of 1974, 5 U.S.C.522a, I hereby request a copy of (or access to) _____(describe as accurately and specifically as possible the record or records you want and provide all the relevant information you have concerning them).

If there are any fees for copying the records I am requesting, please inform me before you fill the request. (Or: please supply the records without informing me if the fees do not exceed $ _____.)

If all or any part of this request is denied, please cite the specific exemption(s) which you think justifies your refusal to release the information. Also, please inform me of your agency's appeal procedure.

In order to expedite consideration of my request, I am enclosing a copy of _____(some document of identification).

Thank you for your prompt attention to this matter.

Signature
Name
Address
City, State, Zip

7

Are Your Finances Confidential?

Next to reading somebody else's love letters, there's nothing quite so delightful as being privy of the facts of his financial life, especially if they tend toward the disastrous.

—*A. C. Spectorsky*

When news reports revealed that Arab interests planned to acquire control of Financial General Bankshares (now known as First American Bankshares), the widely read columnist William Safire wrote that such an acquisition would be "a bonanza for those who might want to influence our nation's opinion leaders and lawmakers." Financial General, which at the time was a $2.2 billion (now over double that amount) financial behemoth, owns a dozen banks in and around Washington, D.C., serving congressmen, government officials, and top military personnel. Safire further observed that if he were a sheik, "the advantages of knowing the financial details of many United States leaders' lives—and the ability to make loans or deny them—would impel [him] toward moving in on the Washington banks." Subsequently, Saudi Arabian interests did acquire effective control.

Government leaders and lawmakers are not the only U.S. citizens with cause to be concerned about the privacy and confidentiality of their financial records. Traditionally, Americans have believed that the details of their personal finances are nobody's business but their own, and have assumed that the confidentiality of information they disclose to banks would be diligently respected and preserved. All too often, this assumption does not conform to practice.

Virtually every American adult is affected by depository and lending institutions. The inconvenience and impracticality of seeking alternative services binds most of us to these organizations. Directly or indirectly, they play key roles in determining whether a person is entitled to receive benefits from a variety of commercial, social, and governmental organizations. Now, with the arrival of electronic funds transfer (EFT), new questions are being raised concerning the adequacy of existing legal protections for the personal records financial institutions maintain on their customers.

A person's banking transactions, particularly the checks that he issues, are a mirror of his life-style, personal interests, and political beliefs. From these records, an interested third party could easily identify the groups he joins and supports, the books and publications he buys, the causes he supports, the material items he purchases, and the personal and political paths he pursues. If an individual applies for a mortgage on his home or for a personal loan to tide him over a short period, the statement of financial condition he would probably be required to fill out would reveal even more intimate financial details. It would include a total rundown of all financial holdings, including stocks and bonds, life insurance, real estate, retirement funds, car, home, and personal property, plus debts and obligations ranging from loans to alimony and child support payments.

Commercial banks, savings and loan associations, mutual savings banks, and credit unions are financial intermediaries acting as go-betweens for suppliers and borrowers of money or for payers and payees. When a person deposits his money, the institution becomes his agent. The primary purpose of records stemming from this relationship is to document the transactions. When someone issues a check, for example, the bank payment is based on that order. The check is the individual's instruction to pay and provides a record to protect both the issuer and the financial institution.

The proliferation of personal banking service records parallels the phenomenal growth of open-end consumer credit over the past few decades. As a result, banks keep a much broader range of records for a much larger portion of the population than they did just a decade ago. This plus the marked increase in personal checking accounts has turned banks into major repositories of information about the activities and relationships of most Americans.

Check Guarantee Service

One of the more recent services of commercial banks that leads to added intrusions into the personal lives of depositors is that of guaranteeing the availability of funds in an individual account. This guarantee helps assure the depositor that his personal checks will be accepted by retailers, while protecting retailers against loss from bad checks. These services, however, do create added risks for banks, and, therefore, bank officials are more selective and inquisitive than in the past about persons who apply to open checking accounts. The application process quite often resembles that of applying for open-end consumer credit. Adverse information supplied by credit-reporting companies could result in the refusal of a bank to open a checking account for you. A full discussion of the banking industry appeared in the U.S. Privacy Protection Commission's report, *Personal Privacy in an Information Society*.

In response to the increase of bad checks, other types of institutions have emerged, which are similar to credit card authorization services. These support organizations maintain information on people who have debts outstanding or who write fraudulent checks.

Because of this expanded activity, a check-guarantee service might include the functions normally handled by depository institutions, credit bureaus, collection agencies, credit card authorization systems, and insurers. This blurring of functions has resulted in some searching and difficult privacy questions. For example, should the individual expect the same rights to his personal information held by the various third-party service organizations with whom he has no direct dealings as he expects for his bank records? Past industry practices and laws have not treated the same personal, sensitive information in the files of different bank-related organizations alike.

How Laws Work and Don't Work

The Currency and Foreign Transactions Reporting Act of 1970 ("Bank Secrecy Act") requires depository organizations to keep certain records on individuals and to report certain types of financial transactions to the government. It was enacted to prevent individuals from evading our laws through the use of secret foreign bank accounts. At the same time, Congress recognized that such records could help in law enforcement, regulation enforcement, and tax administration. Therefore, various government agencies now use the records created by the act for their own administrative purpose.

Financial institutions, dealers, and agents are required to retain a record of credit transactions exceeding $10,000, and to retain documents and instructions relating to transactions in excess of $10,000 where money in its various forms is sent out of the United States. They must report to the Internal Revenue Service any unusual domestic currency transactions involving more than $10,000. Also mandated are reports on the international transportation of currency and certain monetary instruments running over $10,000. A traveler carrying that sum with him must file a report with the U.S. Customs Service when he enters or leaves the United States. The IRS requires any person with a foreign financial account to file a separate schedule describing it along with his federal tax return, and to retain specified records relating to it. One of the most controversial sections is the requirement that all checks of $100 or more be copied and kept for five years. Most banks find that the segregating of checks in excess of $99 for retention is too burdensome, so they microfilm all checks regardless of amount.

The Bank Secrecy Act, which added substantially to the government-accessed records of millions of Americans, has been challenged by bankers and civil libertarians alike on the grounds that it raises fundamental questions about the long-assumed confidentiality between banks and their customers, and between government and individual citizens.

The Right to Financial Privacy Act of 1978 limited some of the broad interpretations of the Bank Secrecy Act by stipulating procedures for federal officials to follow if they want access to bank records. As a general rule, a customer may challenge a government agency's subpoena or formal written request to a financial institution for customer records by filing a motion in a federal district court. Both the agency and the financial institution are liable to pay actual or punitive damages in the event of violation of the act.

The American Bankers Association (ABA), along with the American Civil Liberties Union, has been concerned for some time about the personal privacy issues banks face in complying with the Bank Secrecy Act and other related legislation. In 1985, the ABA told the House Subcommittee on Crime that "the argument that the Right to Financial Privacy Act hinders law enforcement is unfounded." The ABA stated that it would "continue to pursue a policy that balances the legitimate need of law enforcement officials to receive information from financial institutions for legitimate investigative purposes, while preserving our customer's privacy."

The Tax Reform Act of 1976 requires that the Internal Revenue Service provide a taxpayer fourteen days' notice when it issues an administrative summons to see his records at a bank or other financial institution. After receiving this notice, the taxpayer then has a right to intervene in any proceeding with respect to enforcing the summons and may suspend compliance with the summons if he notifies the IRS and the bank within the fourteen-day period. In that case, a federal district judge will decide on whether to enforce the summons. The court may allow the IRS to waive the notice requirement in exceptional circumstances. Credit unions, consumer reporting agencies, credit card companies, brokers, attorneys, and accountants are subject to these same provisions when they are holders of a third party's business records.

Also of note is the Bank Secrecy Act Reports File operated by the Financial Law Enforcement Center. This is a centralized file of certain forms of currency transactions and accounts which are required to be filed under the Bank Secrecy Act. The procedure is intended to facilitate the collection, storage, and retrieval of certain financial information for law enforcement purposes. The accompanying Privacy Act disclosure notice makes it clear that information in the file will be disclosed to federal, state, and local law enforcement agencies and their foreign counterparts to assist in their law enforcement efforts.

The Reality

Most banks try to maintain cooperative relationships with law enforcement agencies and often find it difficult to refuse informal requests for records. An attorney for a California bank gave interesting insights at a hearing held in Washington, D.C., before the U.S. Privacy Protection Commission into the pressures exerted on banks to cooperate with government investigators:

> The normal situation has been for a police officer, an Internal Revenue Agent, or another law enforcement official to appear at a bank branch in person and request certain records relating to a specific customer. . . . Normally the investigating agent will speak with the manager of the branch. If the manager is hesitant in producing the records, the agent will prepare a so-called "pocket summons" and serve it upon the manager. [A pocket summons is merely a blank subpoena signed in advance by a person authorized to do so, with the details to be filled in on the spot when a reluctant bank official is encountered.]
>
> At this point there is pressure upon the bank personnel: (1) to comply with an apparently authorized law enforcement official, and (2) to permit review of the records immediately with the promise, express or implied, that if the bank officer does it will save time and money. This inducement for immediate production is premised upon the representation that the investigating agent by an immediate review can limit the number of records and, if copies are produced, can make it unnecessary for the officer to personally deliver such records to an agency or court at a future date.
>
> These pressures are not inconsiderable. Moreover, it should be borne in mind that the bank official is not a lawyer nor is he or she generally familiar with the statutory and other requirements which apply to determine the validity of such a demand. As a result, in the past, these informal requests and subtle pressures have frequently achieved the objective of the investigating agent and the records have been made available.

In a manual for police captains in one jurisdiction, the captain was advised to get friendly with the local manager of the bank in his area so that when he desired information about a depositor's account, the bank would be more inclined to respond promptly and informally.

Here are some of the kinds of situations bankers run up against everyday:

• A taxpayer is alleged to have omitted substantial earnings from his income tax return—an omission brought to the IRS's attention by an ex-girlfriend. Since his bank transactions could help to complete this case quickly and less expensively for the government, official investigators informally request information in the depositor's bank record.

- A man who had been collecting welfare checks for years on a regular basis is being investigated by a city agency to confirm that he operates an illegal bookie operation producing considerable income. Quiet access to his bank records could help confirm this allegation. The investigator requests a brief examination of the bank records.
- A known criminal represents himself as a retired mechanic. Law enforcement officers are convinced his bank records would provide material to incriminate him by confirming a recent $10,000 deposit and the issuance of a large check to a suspected accomplice. Police officers argue that denying them access to the bank's file would impede law enforcement and make the already difficult task of apprehension and conviction more difficult.

In deciding whether or not to accede to investigators' requests for information, bank officials are put on the spot. It is fairly common practice for financial institutions to exchange information with credit and lending organizations and other private-sector organizations.

Where legitimate channels are not available to third parties, information from individual bank customer records nevertheless may be obtained. Private detectives specializing in the unauthorized capture of such records are adept at an array of techniques, including misrepresentations and financial payoffs. In many states, a bank can legitimately release certain basic information based on its experience with customers. Even where details are not provided, many banks reveal such data as whether balances are in the range of three or four figures.

In a survey of the largest commercial banks in the United States conducted for me by the Survey Research Laboratory at the University of Illinois in 1979, it was revealed that all banks (100%) disclosed information to credit grantors about their depositors and borrowers, and one-fourth (25%) gave information to landlords. But only one in four (24%) obtained authorization of the customer before disclosing this information. However, almost all banks (95%) limited the type of information released to these nongovernment inquirers.

Depositors and borrowers have little knowledge of what their bankers do with the personal financial information that is in their records. Over four out of five (85%) of the largest banks in the nation did not inform their customers of the institution's routine disclosure practices to nongovernmental inquiries, and three out of four (74%) did not inform them of the routine disclosure practices to governmental inquirers. The survey also revealed that over four out of five of the banks responding (82%) did not inform the individual of the types of records maintained on him, use to which these records were put (85%), or which records he has access to (85%).

In another finding, over four out of five banks (82%) verified or supplemented background information collected directly from individuals, but less than half (48%) notified the customers before such information was collected about them. Seven out of ten (72%) did not give the subject access to the information collected.

Although all banks obtained /information from credit bureaus, only about one-third (34%) reviewed the way the bureaus collected the information, how they maintained the records (37%), or what they did about disclosing the information to outside parties (34%). It is encouraging to note that nine of ten banks (91%) had designated an executive-level person for maintaining privacy safeguards in their depository record-keeping practices.

If you have a complaint concerning the handling of your financial records by a financial institution, you should contact that institution's regulatory agency. Complaints concerning banks may be processed through the Federal Deposit Insurance Corporation (FDIC). Address complaints to: Federal Deposit Insurance Corporation, Consumer Affairs Division, 550 17th Street, N.W., Washington, D.C. 20429. The regulatory agency for savings and loan organizations is the Federal Home Loan Bank Board. Complaints should be addressed to: Federal Home Loan Bank Board, Office of Community Investment, 1700 G Street, N.W., Washington, D.C. 20552. Complaints concerning credit unions will be handled by the Federal Credit Union Association (FCUA). Direct inquries to: National Credit Union Association (NCUA), Department of Supervision and Examination, 1776 G Street, N.W., Washington, D.C. 20456.

Although the FDIC and NCUA have toll-free "hotlines" and all three organizations will provide certain information over the telephone, to be acted upon a complaint must be in writing and must contain a signature. Upon receipt of a written complaint, these agencies will contact the institution in question to learn its position. These agencies do possess enforcement authority, and if they determine that your rights have been infringed upon, they will institute measures to correct the problem.

Other Developments

The Federal Reserve District Banks clear checks among the nation's commercial banks and thus play a significant role in the movement of money within the United States. In the past, the confidentiality issue did not arise because the cumbersomeness of the paper chase protected the individual depositor's anonymity. With electronic processing and computer capabilities that facilitate the isolation of individual accounts, the potential for privacy intrusion becomes significant.

As electronic funds transfer (EFT) gains momentum, yet another dimension of performance and procedural information is being sought by governmental agencies. In no way will the amount of information to be furnished decrease, especially as the ability to retrieve details of individual accounts continues to become more and more refined.

Government's reporting requirements, coupled with increasingly intrusive federal and state examiners' auditing procedures, pose additional problems for banks. As a former president of the American Bankers Association put it, "In revealing additional information about bank performance, there clearly is a very real danger of invading the privacy of bank customers."

For decades, the nation's courts in various decisions have recognized that "inviolate secrecy is one of the inherent and fundamental precepts of the relationship of the bank and its customers and depositors" (Peterson v. Idaho First National Bank, 83 Ida, 578, 367 F. 2d 284, 290 [1961]). Nevertheless, the due legal process that laws and the courts have depended upon for protection of the individual have been circumvented by zealous investigators using imaginative techniques.

Evidence indicates that a majority of the nation's banks are genuinely concerned about the sanctity of their depositors' records and are conscientiously cautious when it comes to disclosing individual account information to third-party inquirers. Apart from ethical considerations, their attitude is that policies that avoid problems for depositors also avoid problems for the banks. A number of banks, for example, have procedures requiring government officials to obtain court orders before inspection of a customer's records.

First Amendment rights may be involved when bank records reveal important features of the customer's associations. The customer does not have the opportunity to defend himself against unwarranted access because, in many instances, he is unaware that the third party is seeking access to the records.

Political implications of easy government access to personal and individual records are too disturbing to ignore. It is not realistic to hope that current conditions making it possible for personal privacy violations to occur will be corrected by the system itself. It is equally unrealistic to assume that proper information practices will be followed if controls to prevent circumvention of the system are missing.

The Cashless—and Possibly Faceless—Society

We are at the threshold of a cashless society. In such a society the need for checks and cash will virtually be eliminated by a system that features coded plastic individual debit cards. Electronic terminals strategically located in retail outlets, in the workplace, and even in the home will eliminate the need for trips to the bank. Debit cards are already being used for deposits, withdrawals, and borrowing money, as well as for purchases and payments of bills including taxes.

Until recently POS (point-of-sale) terminals and ATM (automatic teller machine) cards have been organized on a regional basis. For example, California's Interlink is owned by the state's four largest banks and can be accessed from almost 2,300 business locations. Now Visa and MasterCard have jointly introduced Entrée, a debit card that can be used to make purchases by creating instant checking account deductions at any participating retail establishment in the country.

State-of-the-art technology makes debit card transactions almost as fast as using cash. At California's Lucky grocery stores, customers using an ATM card get a receipt listing their purchases along with the date, time, and amount withdrawn from their account. In only 12 to 15 seconds, the entire transaction is completed. Today there are more than 40,000 automatic teller machine (ATM) terminals in use in the United States, and the number of ATMs should exceed 200,000 by 1990. There are over 75,000 ATMs in use worldwide and their growth rate is expected to reach twenty-five percent.

Technology now allows the tracking of bank customers as they go about their daily business. Bank computers can provide a personal profile of a customer's movements and activities that is more timely and detailed than one prepared from an individual's own records.

Electronic funds transfer (EFT) is now operative in many high-traffic locations such as airports and shopping centers, and has replaced payroll checks in many large organizations. Universal adoption of EFT is inevitable, eliminating the burdensome and time-consuming tasks of writing and mailing checks. For financial institutions, the prospect of eliminating check processing is a most attractive lure. It costs at least 27 cents to handle each of the approximately 40 billion checks processed in the United States each year. With EFT, it has been estimated that this cost would be slashed by as much as 80 percent. Two-thirds of all cash transactions also will be replaced by EFT.

With fully functioning EFT, information held by financial institutions about individuals will include more details than in the past. Files will be more easily retrievable than ever before, and some of the records will include information not necessarily relevant as banking data. Transactions are likely to relay information concerning the purpose of the transaction along with dollar amount. Combining payment and administrative information eliminates repetitious paper documentation and avoids duplicate information transfer systems. Under such circumstances, data banks in diverse locations will store information about a person's political leanings, religious affiliations, causes he supports, books and periodicals he reads, travel habits, organizations he belongs to, and purchases he makes. Widespread access to this comprehensive information will have adverse consequences for the confidentiality of that data.

Electronic Fund Transfer Act

The Electronic Fund Transfer Act (Regulation E), enacted in 1980, provides that any institution furnishing electronic transfers or other bank services must notify its customers about third-party access to customer accounts. The banks are also required to make disclosures to customers about their rights and obligations concerning specific EFT transactions, and about whom to contact if they suspect an unauthorized transfer. The act also imposes liabilities on banks for errors in transmission or documentation of transfer. The act, however, is not well known and is poorly enforced.

While this act is an important step forward in building up privacy safeguards in depository institutions, many protections are lacking. More comprehensive fair information practices would inform the bank depositor of the type of information collected about him and how it will be used. He should be permitted to see and copy his file if he wishes, and should be notified if a third party requests information about him. Information generated under an electronic funds transfer system should be retained only in the account records of the financial institutions and other parties to the transaction, and only for as long as is required to fulfill the operational requirements. No government entity should own, operate, or manage an EFT unit that transacts business with private individuals. Government's role should be limited to monitoring such systems for compliance with laws and regulations.

Do State Laws Help Protect Financial Records?

Only five states—New Jersey, South Carolina, Vermont, West Virginia, and Wyoming—lack statutory recognition of financial privacy, and several have legislation regulating the disclosure of an individual's financial records: Alabama, Alaska, California, Connecticut, Illinois, Louisiana, Maryland, New Hampshire, and Oklahoma. States with court decisions acknowledging that financial institutions owe confidentiality to their customers include California, Florida, Idaho, Illinois, Maryland, Minnesota, Missouri, New Jersey, North Carolina, and Washington. Many of the statutes offer procedural safeguards for challenging the disclosure process. California law requires that a bank customer be given a ten-day notice before a state investigator can obtain records concerning the customer's financial affairs from a bank. The customer can challenge the disclosure of his records during the ten-day notification period. The exchange of credit data in the ordinary course of business is authorized under this law. Alaska, Connecticut, Illinois, Louisiana, Maryland, New Hampshire, and Oklahoma have similar laws.

The law in Alabama requires banks to disclose customers' financial records under court order or at the request of a government agency, but notes that customer records should be disclosed only upon legal process.

Court decisions in many states have acknowledged that financial institutions owe confidentiality to their customers and impose some liability for the unauthorized disclosure of customer information. California, Colorado, and Pennsylvania courts have held that bank customers had a reasonable expectation of privacy even though there was no specific statute extending the right to privacy to bank records. In New Hampshire, courts have upheld financial privacy statute violations concerning the issuance of a subpoena or search warrant. A decision in Illinois recognized that a right to financial privacy existed under the Fourth Amendment to the United States Constitution, but held that this right did not extend to reasonable searches and seizures.

Iowa, Florida, and Massachusetts have specifically addressed electronic funds transfer. Iowa prohibits the use of satellite terminals or data-processing centers to obtain information concerning any person's financial institution account, unless such information is essential to complete or prevent the completion of a transaction then being engaged in through the use of that facility. Florida requires banks operating EFTs to inform customers of policies established to prevent the wrongful or accidental disclosure of confidential information, although no specific policies are prescribed. It also prohibits the use of social security numbers as personal identifiers in electronic systems. Massachusetts law states that a provider of electronic funds transfer services may not disclose customer information without prior authorization.

Conclusion

The invasion of an individual's privacy through his financial transactions is very real in America. Data gathered by financial institutions as well as the information that can be gleaned from individual transactions give highly personal details about one's private life. New banking techniques and networking create comprehensive data bases that make prying by official or unofficial intruders much easier.

Although some laws exist that are intended to safeguard individual privacy, these laws are inadequate in scope and are not widely publicized or understood, even by the institutions whose business transactions are governed by them.

We need uniform laws that clearly define the limitations and conditions under which an individual's financial information may be released and to whom it may be released. Banking personnel must be made cognizant of these laws in order to prevent unintended and even unlawful breaches in security.

8

Personal Information that Insurance Companies Need and Get

Knowledge is of two kinds: We know a subject ourselves, or we know where we can find information upon it.

—Samuel Johnson

Well before AIDS came on the scene, "Are you a homosexual?" was a question on an insurance application form.

The insurance company executive testifying before the U.S. Privacy Protection Commission was asked, "Why do you ask that question?"

"If the person is a homosexual, his premium is rated; we charge a higher premium."

"Is that because your actuarial studies show that a homosexual has a shorter life span than a heterosexual?"

"No, we don't have such an actuarial study."

"Then why do you ask the question and charge a higher premium?"

Somewhat taken aback by the question, the insurance executive was momentarily at a loss for words. His attorney spoke up, "We do so because we know that homosexuals generally frequent gay bars. In gay bars rowdyism is more apt to occur, more fights break out. He might get hurt. Therefore, we feel that the premium should be raised."

Using such rationale one could imagine criteria of various unconventional life-style preferences, with insurance questionnaires reflecting these attributes. Inquiries probing moral hazards may cover a person's drinking habits, drug use, credit worthiness, occupational stability, deportment, housekeeping practices, criminal history, and living arrangements. Relevance may not always be easy to demonstrate with judgment often left to the underwriter handling a particular case.

Socrates counseled, "There is only one good, that is knowledge; there is only one evil, that is ignorance." The average person has little knowledge regarding the practices of the insurance industry, and therefore a great deal of ignorance regarding his personal vulnerability. Your insurance company representatives need and get a great deal of medical, financial, and social information about you—much more than you furnish them. How do they get it? How accurate is it? What do they do with it? Who else sees it?

When you apply for insurance, you are required to sign an authorization statement. This gives the insurer and its support personnel authority to get information about you from virtually any source they may wish. The waiver most applicants routinely sign has been characterized as "a search warrant without due process."

Too many authorizations contain no expiration date. No limits are specified regarding the investigative scope or information sources that may be questioned. Often no satisfactory explanation is given to help you understand what it is you are consenting to, and any copy of the authorization may be as valid as the original. A survey of major insurance companies conducted at my request by the Survey Research Laboratory at the University of Illinois a number of years ago revealed that two out of five insurance application authorization forms contained no expiration date, nor did they name what information was sought or how it would be used. Forty percent of the companies disclosed the information they obtained to others without customer permission. A recent poll found that a majority of psychiatrists believed that confidentiality of their patients' records is breached by insurance companies, and that their patients did not realize what they did when they signed the blanket consent form.

In part because the authorization forms applicants sign for employment or insurance are broadly worded, the role played by investigative firms who use the authorizations is not generally understood by the public. What is more, to the extent that investigative bureaus rely on information in their own files in making reports, they can play a gatekeeping role that significantly affects an individual's relationships with many organizations. Where adverse information is kept on file for many years, the subject may not be able to avoid having this information furnished to others when inquiries are made about him. Such conditions present dangers of unfair and damaging stigmatization. When adverse decisions occur with no apparent justificiation, constant inquiry into the content of a record-keeping organization's files should be the guiding principle.

When signing any authorization statement on any application form in order for the holder to obtain information about you with your permission, ask to strike out portions which permit unlimited access to and dissemination of information unrelated to the service sought.

The applicant entering into an insurance transaction usually has no idea how extensive or intrusive the information-gathering process will be. It was encouraging to learn from our survey some time ago that 80 percent of the companies gave insureds access to personal information in the company's files.

Some applications state that information not only from the application itself, but also from the underwriting investigation conducted in the insurer's behalf may be reported to the insurance industry-sponsored Medical Information Bureau (MIB). (A discussion of MIB follows, below.) Considering the practices of some investigative firms, this could have serious implications for the applicant who cannot always weigh the relative benefits of the insurance coverage against the costs and hazards of making his private data available to others. Unless he takes the initiative at least with those four out of five companies that allow access to information compiled about him, he is not able to correct or amend any data that might be false or inaccurate. Of course, applicants for coverage with the one out of five companies that do not permit access have no such opportunity.

Apart from the immediate consequences of an adverse decision, incorrect information may continue to stigmatize the individual well into the future. Some insurers have been known to use the fact of a previous declination of coverage by another insurer as a basis for rejecting the applicant. One out of five companies revealed that its application acceptance decision was based on another company's prior determination. This might be economically justified on the premise that "if he failed to meet Insurer A's requirements, he'll probably fail to meet ours as well," however, the previous turndown may have had no bearing on the person's current qualifications. In some cases, for example, an applicant may be declined simply because he happens to live outside of the insurer's predetermined area of preferred concentration.

There is little doubt that the insurance industry has a clear and valid need for personal information about the people it insures. It must know a person's medical history in order to know the risk of insuring him. It also has to protect itself against would-be profiteers who file fraudulent claims. When policy holders misrepresent the facts and are awarded more than they deserve in settlements, insurance premiums are raised for everyone.

Insurance physical examinations are becoming more encompassing. The 1986 drug-related death of basketball star Len Bias has focused attention on the drug problem. Insurers such as the Los Angeles–based Transamerican Occidental Life Insurance Company recently began testing for cocaine usage among applicants for large life insurance policies. Cocaine is detectable for forty-eight hours after use. "If someone can't get off it for that period of time, you probably have a serious problem there," according to W. Taylor Fiederlein of North American Reassurance Company, New York.

To what extent does this legitimate need for information impinge on privacy rights? At first glance it is difficult to sympathize with a multibillion-dollar industry when matched against the resources of an inexperienced individual trying to protect himself against intrusions to his privacy. The match is clearly lopsided. As one insurance executive observed, "The company-agent system works toward the benefit of the company, not the customer." There is no effective advocacy system for customers of insurance companies. Individual clients must fend for themselves.

A Denver, Colorado, grand jury probe revealed how a service bureau conducted its operations in illegally obtaining medical records. The company advertised that it could provide records without authorization to insurance companies to cut their costs. The company's investigators obtained medical files by posing as doctors or nurses or by paying hospital employees to obtain desired information not authorized to be released. The district attorney bringing charges against the firm argued that many insurance companies closed their eyes to the practices of those they engaged to perform investigative services for them.

Medical Information Bureau—The Industry's Major Source

Insurance companies have an impressive array of legitimate industry resources to feed their need for information. The largest of these is the Medical Information Bureau (MIB), an industry association which gathers, processes, and disseminates data relating to the insurance policies of over twelve million people.

MIB's basic purpose is to "detect and deter fraud and misrepresentation in connection with the underwriting of life and health insurance and claims," according to its 1984 Factsheet. The system relies on a confidential interchange of underwriting information among its members to ferret out fraudulent applications and claims, and hence to protect the honest consumers from having to pay higher premium costs. MIB claims that "only member companies may have access to MIB's record information; it is not released to non-member companies, to credit or consumer reporting agencies, or to government agencies who do not have a court order or authorization from the consumer."

About eight hundred U.S. and Canadian life insurers are MIB members, and each of these members generates information for the bureau's use. Any time one company uncovers what it considers significant information about an individual, it codes it with a general label and feeds it to the bureau. Another member company will normally check with the bureau when it receives a life insurance application. If the applicant has ever been denied insurance, or coded for any reason, the inquiring company will learn of it and, theoretically, go directly to the original company for details. In fact, however, there is no assurance that an inquiring company will investigate further before rejecting an applicant, even though MIB neither verifies nor investigates the information it disseminates. Furthermore, MIB requires its members to report information regardless of how it was acquired. The bureau allows individuals access to their records and has a procedure for correction in accordance with the Fair Credit Reporting Act, but few people know about their rights. Of the 12 million medical histories in the MIB files, about 7,000 persons request disclosure each year, and 200 ask for corrections.

MIB does have rules about how its information should be used, but those rules are difficult to enforce. The system ultimately relies on the faith that the code will be respected and that an insurer will not base an adverse underwriting decision solely upon MIB information. Unfortunately, this does not always happen, and qualified individuals are sometimes unfairly denied insurance. When this occurs, both parties suffer. The individual doesn't get the insurance he wants and the insurance company loses business.

A Variety of Other Sources

There are a number of other sources of personal information to which insurance companies can turn. The Impairment Bureau reports on life and health insurance applicants who have been denied coverage. The Loss Indexes are maintained by the American Insurance Association and reveal whether a claimant has had a series of prior losses or is submitting claims for the same loss to more than one company. The indexes cover fire, burglary or theft, fine arts losses, and third-party personal or bodily injury claims arising under automobile, homeowners, malpractice, and worker's compensation policies.

Records on reported fire losses are maintained by the National Fire Incident Reporting System (NFIRS), a computerized data base maintained in Emmitsburg, Maryland, by the United States Fire Administration and the National Fire Information Council. Currently, fire departments in approximately forty-two states participate in the loss-reporting system. The findings are published as public information. Although this information does not list specific names and addresses, it does indicate fire losses and incidents within a specific area.

The National Automobile Theft Bureau investigates fraudulent claims of theft, fire, or fraud losses and develops programs to minimize these losses. It also operates as a national clearinghouse for stolen-car information. To help combat vehicle crime, the bureau maintains over 3.5 million on-line records in its North American Theft Information System (NATIS). These records are immediately accessible from remote terminals located across the country. The NATIS computer index currently contains information on motor vehicle theft, including aircraft and boats, salvage, and arson. In order to track a vehicle from "birth to death," the bureau is comtemplating collecting data on claims involving automobile liability (including uninsured motorists); liability other than automobile, including liability claims under homeowners, commercial, multiple peril, pleasure craft, and aircraft policies; claims based on false arrest, assault and battery, or malpractice claims; and worker's compensation claims. The Insurance Crime Prevention Institute (ICPI) seeks to uncover insurance fraud for property and liability insurers.

Life insurance in force in the United States amounted to nearly $6,700 billion at the end of 1986, according to Barbara Blunt of the American Council of Life Insurance. A national consumer survey conducted by the Life Insurance Marketing and Research Association found that 70% of adults in the United States owned some type of life insurance. The number of U.S. life insurance companies in business in 1986 was estimated at 2,260, employing nearly 2 million people. In addition, 46 million Americans were covered by pension plans with life insurance companies. Pension plans totaled 5.5 million. Over 90% of the nation's registered automobiles are insured, and few homes are without insurance coverage.

Because life insurance is often sold as part of a financial-planning package offered by agents, an applicant may divulge a good deal of personal information about himself even before the application is completed. For example, when insurance is tied to estate conservation, the agent collects detailed information about the prospect's net worth, income, family relationships, career prospects, personal life-style, and goals. Some life insurance agents have more comprehensive knowledge about a client's financial and personal affairs than members of the applicant's own family.

The primary sources of information in life and health underwriting are the applicant and the agent. But because each has a financial stake in the sale, outside investigators are often used to check the accuracy and completeness of information provided. In verifying application information, investigators contact employers, associates, bankers, neighbors, and creditors. They get information from hospitals and clinics, check public records for evidence of legal or financial difficulties, and contact third-party sources such as doctors, accountants, and lawyers who have a confidential relationship with the applicant.

In property and liability coverage, the insurer wants to know enough about the applicant to make a reasonably accurate appraisal of his probable loss characteristics. In the case of automobile insurance, for example, the underwriter wants to know if those using the car are responsible drivers.

In one case, the application form for automobile liability insurance inquired whether the applicant lived in cohabitation with another person. When I challenged the executive of the insurance company during his testimony before the USPPC for asking such a question, because of what appeared to be its irrelevance, the response fully justified the need for the question to be asked. He explained, "It's not irrelevant at all. You see, the automobile liability insurance premium rate for a married person is higher than for a single person because we know that an automobile is used by both spouses. We also know from experience that when people live in cohabitation, even if not married, both parties will also share use of that same automobile. Therefore, the insurance rate has to be more comparable to the higher, married rate than if the insured were living alone."

Supply and Demand

Information gathering and disclosure has become a multimillion dollar industry. The supply keeps growing in response to the demands by insurers and employers who base dollar decisions on what they can learn about clients, applicants, and employees.

Without creditable information, the insurer would be unable to evaluate the risk it is being asked to assume in order to set premium charges that are fair in relation to anticipated losses and claims. As a consequence, the innocent client would be penalized by dishonest applications and fraudulent claims through the higher insurance rates passed on to all policyholders.

Sometimes an investigator's overzealous practices result in unfair activities. In one case, a woman answering her telephone was greeted with, "I am doing advertising for a company that manufacturers detergents. May I ask what detergent you use in your washing machine?"

The woman responded, naming the brand.

"Well, that's just fine. We're preparing a TV commercial for that same brand. May we come to your home while you're doing your wash so that we can take pictures of it?"

Obviously pleased, imagining herself pictured in national advertising, the woman invited the callers to her home where they photographed her doing the weekly laundry. The only time she saw the pictures was in court when a corporate lawyer was contesting her claim that she had injured her back in an automobile accident and was unable to perform household chores.

Legal control and oversight of the insurance industry is exercised at the state level. It stresses two basic aims: (1) to maintain the solvency of individual insurance companies; and (2) to ensure fair business practices and pricing. For the most part, inadequate attention has been paid to problems of fair information practice. What is more, the control of record-keeping practices at the state level is limited with state insurance departments lacking regulatory authority over most insurance "support" organizations.

"I'm so sorry to hear you have cancer."

A middle-aged woman, hospitalized for a tumor, learned that it was malignant and began receiving chemotherapy treatments. Returning to work a few weeks later, she was edgy, anxious, and extremely sensitive regarding her condition. She did not want others to know about her illness fearing they would treat her as an object of pity. Yet on her very first day back at work following her confinement she was stopped on the way to her desk by a sympathetic co-worker. "I'm so sorry to hear you have cancer," the other employee remarked.

The patient's medical record was on file in the personnel office because the employer administered a group health policy. Easily accessible, the entire staff learned of her condition.

Unfortunately, this is not an isolated example. Millions of Americans are covered by group programs of all types. Some employers use information in these records to decide if a person should be promoted or even retained in employment. There is no federal prohibition to prevent this kind of access or use. As a matter of fact, in our survey reported in Chapter 4, 50 percent of the companies used medical records "in making employment-related decisions."

Medical Information and Insurance Records

Several years ago, the American Psychiatric Association (APA) Task Force on Confidentiality prepared a sampling of typical case histories to demonstrate the damage potential inherent in unauthorized disclosure of medical records. Here are a couple of typical cases that were reported:

> A 24-year-old schizophrenic patient, receiving EST in hospital[,] improved and was able to return to work. Patient not told actual diagnosis because of still fragile state. Insurance covered patients routinely are given forms to sign on hospital admission. Includes permission to give information to insurance company. Hospital sent a report of hospitalization as routine matter to get payment for bill, including diagnosis of suicide attempt. On return to work, patient found that fellow employees know of the hospitalizations, the incidents. Insurance company sends report to employer on group contract coverage. Patient becomes paranoid toward her physician; expresses self about first learning about herself from fellow employees; terminates treatment.

> A very emotionally upset patient, first making inquiries from insurance company that no information would reach employer, was so assured. The entire therapy is damaged when the patient finds employer discloses knowledge of the treatment and other factors. Medical director of the national company involved and a high official in insurance organizations writes "we are obligated to tell the employer because he pays the premiums." (Note that such group contracts are fringe benefits paid for by employees' labor, and are only administratively paid for by employer.)

In an August 1987 interview conducted by my research assistant with Dr. Jerome S. Beigler, former Chairman of the American Psychiatric Association Committee on Confidentiality, he noted, "Because of the stigma attached to some medical treatment, many patients who have paid for health insurance by direct premiums or indirectly by their work, realistically dare not avail themselves of such benefits lest their immediate employment and/or future careers be impaired. Civil service employees, military personnel, corporate executives, politicians, and teachers are known not to use their insurance lest they be on record as having been in psychiatric treatment." One patient was an aide to a top federal official in Chicago. The patient paid for his treatment instead of using available insurance. "He did not want to take any chance of people finding out about the treatment," Beigler explained, "because he had ambitions of being prominent federally some day." Another patient was a middle-level advertising executive with ambitions for promotion.

According to Beigler, the problem of medical treatment confidentiality has been exacerbated in recent years due to an increasing number of small and medium-sized businesses processing insurance claims in-house. Beigler says that the advent of computers has made it easier for employers to keep tabs on employees' utilization of insurance benefits.

All psychiatrists are aware of the problems of confidentiality. Many members of the APA subscribe to a legal consultant service in Washington, D.C., and the most commonly asked questions concern confidentiality. Dr. Beigler reported that in a survey of the Illinois and Michigan chapters of the American Psychiatric Association 75 percent of psychiatrists knew of patients who had not used their health insurance. Eighty percent of the psychiatrists surveyed said the issue was important, that patients were afraid to use insurance to pay for psychiatric treatment.

One Maryland physician found that in a twelve-year period, those of his patients who ignored their Blue Cross health insurance coverage paid a total of $168,075 out of their own pockets for psychiatric care, or an average of over $14,000 a year for one physician's patients alone.

Employees have a right to fear their employer's finding out about psychiatric treatment paid for by group insurance. Dr. Douglas Sargeant, Chairman of the APA Committee on Confidentiality and a Detroit psychiatrist, said the workplace is a "very important facet of the problem of confidentiality." Speaking in a 1987 interview with my research assistant, Sargeant said, "It has been our experience that some insurers leak information to the employers with the hope of reducing claims, [because] the claims process [is made] onerous and creates in employees justifiable fear that if they draw on the benefit they will be sanctioned or fired."

Dr. Sargeant gave an example of what can happen if the boss finds out about a medical record without checking it with the employee. "One man I know who suffered from depression overcame his fear of seeking help and went to a psychiatrist," Dr. Sargeant said. "He was told by the personnel office that his claim would be kept confidential, but within a month his boss had found out about it and he was fired."

In another case, a woman clerk quit after someone saw on her group insurance forms that she was being treated for schizophrenia. A man receiving therapy for alcoholism resumed drinking after a lecture from his personnel manager who found out about the treatment.

A patient who is a very high official in a large financial institution paid cash for his psychiatric treatment because if this had been made known in his workplace it would have affected his advancement opportunities.

One way to correct this problem, according to medical authorities, is to bypass the employer's personnel office by sending insurance claims directly to the carrier's office where personnel are not coworkers of the patient and are more likely to be trained to maintain confidentiality. The International Business Machines Corporation has successfully implemented medical-information privacy protection by this means. The only data the employer receives are periodic statistical analyses without any individuals identified.

It is interesting to note that both Dr. Beigler and Dr. Sargeant say some insurance companies are known to urge employers to run claim forms through personnel departments rather than through the insurance company. "This puts pressure [on the employees] and makes employees not comfortable about using their insurance," Dr. Beigler explained.

The American Psychiatric Association has also warned of the considerable threat to confidentiality posed by large, computerized information networks. The association's Committee on Confidentiality addressed the problem in its "Guidelines on Confidentiality," which said, "When the record itself is computerized, either in the office, the clinic or the hospital, extreme care should be taken to guard against inappropriate access to the information contained. Whatever the system of safeguards installed, it is wise to test that it is 'leak-proof' with regard to confidentiality by having an outside expert challenge it." The guidelines suggest that once medical data enters a "non-medical information system" it is vulnerable to unwarranted access and inappropriate use.

Disclosure requirements for insurance coverage sometimes force a doctor to release confidential information. It is not uncommon for an insurance company claim monitor to call a hospital to get detailed medical data in order to check on progress and future need of treatment of an insured patient. Hospital charge forms, Dr. Sargeant observes, often request the doctor to inform the patient's employer of the condition of the patient. Dr. Sargeant sees such disclosure regulations as threats to personal privacy. He says the privacy issue is "a problem that is getting more play right now. Increasing numbers of people are trying to protect their rights of claiming benefits."

The APA would like the insurance industry to use informed consent rather than blanket disclosure authorizations on contracts. It is convinced that many people do not always understand or are unaware of the blanket disclosure authorization they must sign to gain insurance coverage or obtain some other benefits. The APA has also recommended that insurance claims be routed to medical claims departments of insurance companies rather than through the personnel offices of employers. However, Dr. Sargeant admitted, "The APA has not been very muscular in getting the insurance industry to change."

When an insurance company is also an employer, there is a potential conflict of interest. A New York insurance salesman and his wife went to a marriage counselor and filed a claim with his insurance company/employer. The counselor wrote down details about the man's mental condition on the claim form. The claim was turned down and the company then fired the salesman on the basis of the information on the form, arguing that the employee had hidden a mental condition when applying for the job. The employee sued under New York's human rights law and won nearly $10,000 in an out-of-court settlement.

Insurance carriers provide a unique service in protecting the average citizen against unforeseen financial losses by spreading the economic burden among the many. To render this service requires enough information about you to be able to make fair judgments concerning the risks being assumed. Obviously, this necessitates careful probing into many sensitive, personal areas to an extent greater than that conducted by any other industry.

In an insurance relationship, the two basic privacy questions are: Is the insured informed of the extent of the searching probes that will be made by the insurance company? and Are there adequate protections to assure that the data collected is fully protected from use other than that for which it was originally obtained? Indications suggest that although some leaders in the industry have highly effective procedures in place, for all too many companies, much remains to be done in both areas.

State Legislative Actions

In 1980, the National Association of Insurance Commissioners issued the *Information and Privacy Protection Model Act* which was intended to serve as a basic state insurance law. This model, revised in 1981, contained a number of crucial protections for the individual insurance policyholder, including: the requirement that insurers provide a notice of information practices to all applicants or policyholders; restrictions on the use of pretext interviews; stipulations on the content and expiration of disclosure authorization forms;

a specification of where those disclosures may be made; provisions for access and correction of records; and a requirement that the individual should be informed about the reasons for any adverse underwriting decision. These guidelines are based on the fair information principles recommended by the U.S. Privacy Protection Commission.

At least ten states (Arizona, California, Connecticut, Georgia, Hawaii, Illinois, Montana, North Carolina, Oregon, and Virginia) have enacted privacy protection laws based on this model. Seven other states have adopted limited insurance privacy protection laws. Louisiana law entitles a patient to receive any information sent to an insurance company by a health-care provider. South Carolina provides that an insurance company must specify reasons for cancellation of auto liability insurance upon request. Such notice is deemed privileged communication. New Jersey authorizes a hospital utilization review committee to provide information on any patient to an insurance company as long as the terms of the policy permit this transaction. Maryland requires that medical files compiled by insurance companies shall be available for inspection upon demand by the subject of the file, and such information may not be revealed to third parties, except with the individual's authorization. In Kansas, insurance companies must inform applicants or policyholders of the reasons for an adverse decision to insure or pay a claim along with the sources of information used by the company. Georgia law prohibits pretext interviews by investigators. Also, insurance companies must follow certain procedures of fairness when gathering information about individuals. In Maine, insurance companies are barred from asking applicants to reveal whether they have been tested for the AIDS virus. Here, as in many other areas of sensitive personal data, protective laws and procedures are spotty, without effective federal monitoring.

Conclusion

The insurance industry, due to the nature of its business, requires a great deal of personal information about its clients. Much of this information is obtained on the application form or through personal interviews, medical examinations, and private investigations. Means of gaining such information is not always ethical or legal. Sometimes an insurance applicant must weigh his need for insurance benefits against damage the unintended use of the revealed personal data might have on his personal life and career.

To obtain information, insurance companies require applicants to sign blanket authorizations, engage professional investigators, and use third parties whose statements may not always be reliable. Often information is not verified, resulting in denial of insurance coverage, as well as other hardships. Laws which govern the gathering and protection of information used by the insurance industry are relegated to the states. Some states have instituted fairly adequate measures, but many have not adopted appropriate legislation. Laws need to be more comprehensive, covering personal privacy protections in all their dimensions.

9

Credit: The Record-Keeping Explosion

A university colleague of mine and his wife were browsing in an automobile dealer's showroom that they had entered for the first time, and they paused in front of a model that appealed to them. A salesman approached, introduced himself, and began describing the various features. After ten minutes, the salesman excused himself, but shortly returned to continue the sales pitch with considerable enthusiasm. Noting a flash of interest on the part of the prospective purchaser, the salesman took the keys out of the car, handed them to him saying, "Inasmuch as you appear to like what you see, here are the keys. The car is yours. You can take it home now after signing our basic sales form."

Taken aback, my colleague reminded the salesman that they had just met. He asked how the salesman could trust a purchaser with a new car simply on his signature, without knowing any more about him. The salesman escorted my colleague to a small office off the showroom floor containing a computer terminal. There he typed into the computer the name of the purchaser and instantly there flashed onto the screen his full credit, financial, and earnings history. My colleague was surprised and upset.

When he reached home, he telephoned me and in a tense voice exclaimed, "How could a total stranger possibly have all that information on me? Who else has access to it and what do they do with it? Where do they get it? I've always been so discreet about those to whom I disclose my personal affairs. Now I begin to understand what the work of the Privacy Protection Commission was all about."

The consumer reporting bureau, the source of the data flashed onto the computer terminal in the automobile showroom, functions as a clearinghouse, or centralized source, for information supplied by credit grantors, collection agencies, and its own culling of public records. Though in existence for almost a century, the expansion of open-end credit coupled with computer, telecommunication, and account-monitoring technology has increased the credit bureau's significance in the overall credit system.

Consumer reporting bureaus are depositories of personal credit histories on most Americans, yet few of us have any direct contact with them. The information in their files about you that they distribute to their subscribers may determine whether you get that job, bank loan, or credit card. Where do they get the data? How reliable is it? Can you see it?

There are approximately 1,200 credit bureaus in operation in the U.S. today. This number represents a significant drop since the late 1970s due to a gradual acquisition of smaller firms by the nation's major credit bureaus. The majority of this number are either affiliated with or owned by five major companies: Equifax, TRW, Trans Union, Chilton, and CSC Credit Services. As a result, most credit records in existence in the United States are held in five massive computers.

Data on an individual and his or her spouse typically include: identifying information—usually name, social security number, address, and telephone number; financial status and employment information, including income; credit history, such as types of credit granted, credit grantors, and payment data; existing lines of credit, payment habits, and outstanding debts; public-record information, pertinent newspaper clippings, arrest and conviction records, bankruptcies, tax liens, and lawsuits; and a listing of bureau subscribers that have requested credit reports on the individual.

Although credit grantors are a credit bureau's principal subscribers, information is also made available to collection agencies, insurance companies, employers, landlords, and law enforcement agencies. While credit reports account for the main revenue of most credit bureaus, some also provide computerized "pre-screening" of mailing lists used for marketing purposes. Some of the larger bureaus offer an account-monitoring service which automatically warns a subscriber if activity in an individual's file warrants reexamination for credit worthiness.

Changes in credit-granting methods and increased automation have spawned new forms of credit reporting. Much of this change has occurred since passage of the Fair Credit Reporting Act, which has had an important impact on the industry. That act, among other things, permits a rejected applicant to request the reason for an adverse credit decision—a procedure which will be explained later in this chapter. The credit card programs of commercial banks are essentially open-end loans of no predetermined amount. These programs are being used more extensively and have redefined the credit risk, which must now be measured by the total amount of credit available to an individual rather than the amount of debt he is already carrying. Extensive investigation into an individual's financial history is required to establish an appropriate credit limit. This limit is determined after an examination of an applicant's past credit history, income, and consumer habits. Much of this information is acquired from sources other than the applicant himself.

Commercial Reporting Services

Commercial credit grantors, like consumer credit grantors, collect information from and about business applicants in order to evaluate their credit worthiness. When a business applies for credit, personal information about the individuals involved in the business may be collected and evaluated in deciding whether to grant or deny credit to the business establishment. Dun and Bradstreet (D&B) is a leading provider of this type of service, selling the information it gathers on an enterprise's current condition and future prospects.

Like consumer reporting agencies, commercial agencies gather information about applicants from a wide variety of sources. Unlike consumer reporting agencies, however, commercial reporting services are not subject to the Fair Credit Reporting Act. Thus, individuals and firms about whom they collect information cannot avail themselves of the act's existing protections against unfair record-keeping and disclosure practices. In order to evaluate the condition of a business enterprise, highly personal information is often collected and recorded about the principals themselves.

In one instance, a self-employed businessman applied for an insurance policy. "A woman came to the house," he recalled. "She talked to me and said she would talk to some of my neighbors. Just routine. Not to worry."

Soon afterward, he started worrying. "The insurance company rejected me cold," he said. "I ran over there and they told me about some report that I'd been mixing dog food in the prepared food I sold in food stores. The report also claimed that my franchise had been closed for a year by the health department. Unbelievable, but that wasn't all. Seventeen years earlier, a girl and I had gotten into trouble. The technical charge was statutory rape, though no rape was involved. I paid a fine and, as a juvenile, the record supposedly was sealed. Now the insurance report said I'd been convicted of rape. But that wasn't all.

"The investigator reported my wife and I had been dealing in drugs. That we held wild parties. The investigator hadn't liked my appearance, either. She made a big thing of how, when interviewed, I'd come to the door 'naked to the waist' (the temperature was over 100 degrees that day). She also said my wife and I were alcoholics. We couldn't believe all this was happening. I learned the investigator worked for a credit bureau. I'd never heard of them, but I sued, and instead of retracting the report they fought like tigers." A federal judge awarded the businessman $42,000 in damages, plus $7,500 for legal fees. To avoid an appeal by the company, on advice of his lawyer the businessman settled for $20,000.

Error in Consumer Reporting

Although the Fair Credit Reporting Act requires credit bureaus to have "reasonable procedures" to assure the accuracy of information reported to subscribers, disturbing errors nevertheless do occur. In one case, a New York resident was embarrassed before his friends when he tried to use his credit card to pay for New Year's Eve festivities. Not only was he denied credit, but his card was confiscated as well. The response of the credit card company to the cardholder's complaint was, "Your remittance was posted to another account in error. This will be corrected in your next statement." Only after the company corrected its own error was the card returned.

When the individual has the determination to learn the true reason an application for credit or service is turned down and to challenge it, frequently there are surprising revelations. A case that has become a classic example of how wrong information in a file can result in serious, harmful consequences to an individual concerns a journalist who had moved from Washington, D.C., to assume a higher post with his same employer in St. Louis. After he applied for automobile insurance, a policy was set up for him by the insurance company. Shortly thereafter the policy was cancelled because of information revealed in a consumer credit report.

Surprised and disturbed because he did not have a poor driving record and had never been in an accident, the journalist investigated. His visit to the office of the credit reporting company revealed in part: "The file shows that you are very much disliked by your neighbors at that location [the journalist's Washington residence] and were considered to be a 'hippy type.' The file indicated that you participated in many demonstrations in Washington, D.C., and that you also housed out-of-town demonstrators. The file indicates that these demonstrators slept on floors, in the basement, and wherever else there was room on your property. The file shows that you were strongly suspected of being a drug user by neighbors, but they could not positively substantiate these suspicions. You are known to have had shoulder-length hair and a beard on one occasion while living in Washington, D.C."

Shocked, the newspaperman disputed virtually all of the information and demanded an explanation of several of the allegations. Finally he sued. During the course of the legal process, he learned about critical comments concerning his wife that were included in his file along with other derogatory allegations. One of the documents introduced at the trial was an excerpt from a handbook issued to each branch manager of the credit reporting company:

The important thing is to NEVER check the files in the presence of the consumer. . . . Prior to the time of your appointment with the consumer, you will have received the Statement of Disclosure from the Home Office. At the time of your appointment any and all information you may have relating to the consumer, such as copies of files, a copy of your statement, index cards, etc., are to be in your desk drawer out of SIGHT of the consumer. You are not to show anything or acknowledge that you have anything other than the Statement of Disclosure.

Actual disclosure will be accomplished by reading the Statement of Disclosure to the consumer. The Statement is to be read word for word at your normal reading speed. It is not to be read slow enough for anyone to copy down word for word, nor is it to be read so fast that the consumer will not understand what you are saying. Part or all of the Statement of Disclosure may be reread if the consumer indicates he did not understand what you were saying. The consumer and/or the person with him may not have a copy of the Statement, nor may they be allowed to read the Statement or touch it.

All of the information in the journalist's file purportedly came from one neighbor—an elderly woman—who had a grudge against the newspaperman because he was sympathetic to antiwar demonstrators and because his children played on her lawn, occasionally destroying her flower beds. It was further revealed that the investigator averaged seventy to eighty reports a week and spent from ten to thirty minutes on each insurance investigation.

The journalist's character, reputation in the community, working habits, personal life-style, and family relationships were testified to by character witnesses of national reputation at the trial. The court found that the credit-reporting company's investigator had "knowingly included false information in the report," and that "methods of reporting on consumers' credit backgrounds as shown at the trial were so slipshod and slovenly as to not even approach the realm of reasonable standards of care imposed by the statute." The journalist was granted $2,500 in actual damages, $25,000 in punitive damages, and $14,000 in attorney's fees.

After this case had been given considerable exposure, the national consumer reporting company involved indicated that it had changed its policies to incorporate fair information practices. Clearly, the victim had to go to considerable trouble and expense to track down the reason behind the adverse decision and to seek justice. How many other people have been and are being harmed by equivalent circumstances, but lack the means, determination, or persistence to seek redress?

A lawyer who advised his clients to regularly check their credit records decided to check his own one day. Richard Brudzynski asked the Credit Bureau of Cleveland for permission to see his file, and the clerk told him he was married. Being single, he wanted to find out the name of his "wife," which turned out to be Florence Brudzynski, his mother's name. The file also showed that he used to work as an attorney for the Cleveland firm of Rudd,

Karl, Sheerer and Lybarger and currently worked as a stockboy for Aeromotive Industries. Brudzynski still worked for the law firm and had not been a stockboy for more than five years.

In another case, a woman was denied automobile insurance because a credit company report indicated that she regularly drank to excess, entertained men in her home, and was otherwise of "low morals." After learning her application was denied, she visited the credit office to look at her file. She was told about only part of the report's contents, and when she challenged its accuracy, the company refused to reinvestigate. She composed a rebuttal statement which was included in her file, but when a subsequent report was sent to her existing insurance carrier, her policy was cancelled. After a great deal of distress, inconvenience, and an agonizing trial, a jury determined that the report was untrue, and her litigation was successful.

It might be noted that a major credit bureau reported that one-third of all consumers who examine their files find mistakes, although most are minor. If you do suspect that your file contains false information and you do not get satisfaction directly from your creditor or the credit bureau involved, before you file a lawsuit contact Associated Credit Bureaus, Inc. (ACB). This Houston-based organization does not have enforcement power, but will be glad to mediate a dispute between a consumer and a credit bureau.

Bill Detlefson, Public Relations Officer for ACB, defines the organization's role as one of "re-establishing communications." He estimates that 90 percent of the time communication is the source of the difficulty and this problem can be overcome by means short of costly litigation.

The following disclaimer appears on most credit reports: "This information is furnished in response to an inquiry for the purpose of evaluating credit risk. It has been obtained from sources deemed reliable, the accuracy of which this organization does not guarantee. The inquirer has agreed to indemnify the reporting bureau for any damage arising from misuse of this information and this report is furnished in reliance upon that indemnity. It must be held in strict confidence, it must not be revealed to the subject reported on, except by a reporting agency in accordance with the Fair Credit Reporting Act." Such disclaimers, however, do not restrain the users of the credit report from giving the contents full credibility in making decisions about the subject.

Bases for Error Vary Widely

Testifying before Congress, one former investigator for a consumer credit-reporting company described a procedure known as "zinging": "A zing means you do nothing. You do not contact the investigatee. . . . One does not go out on the street. . . . He utilizes whatever information was supplied by the insurance company, and, hopefully, looks up the insured in the phone book to assure that he lives there; then you just fill in the form." Another investigator for the same company described "the crystal-ball system" which "consists of quoting old reports, looking at the information on an inquiry, and determining that the individual 'looks okay.' " These practices, of course, are denied by industry executives. It also has been alleged that some credit-reporting companies give their investigators such high daily and weekly quotas that they are forced to take shortcuts in order to complete their assignments on time.

The Federal Trade Commission found it necessary to order one agency to abandon its quota system of "quality control audits" which encouraged investigators to produce a percentage of negative reports. An employee of that company testified that he had fabricated the number of times that persons under investigation had engaged in "excessive drinking." A federal appeals court concluded that although no violation of the law had been proven, the agency's policies did encourage investigators to come up with adverse information.

In an exchange between the then Congressman Edward Koch and a senior executive of one of the largest consumer reporting companies in the nation, the dialogue went as follows:

QUESTION: Do you assure your sources that their names will not be revealed?

ANSWER: Yes, we do assure them that their name will not be revealed and that they are giving the information to us in confidence. There is a confidential assurance and confidential relationship between us and our source of information. . . .

Q: In your judgment, does that encourage something less than full integrity? (If, for example, the individual being interviewed happens to have a grudge against his neighbor.)

A: No. To the contrary, our experience has been that this more nearly insures full integrity and objectivity as opposed to any other system. If we took the contrary route and said we must of necessity reveal the source of our information, then there would not be a free and full flow of information.

Q: What kind of control exists to see to it that certain kinds of basic information that were never intended to be disclosed do not get into the files because of an over-ambitious or misdirected employee?

A: We very carefully supervise the work of each individual through his work supervisor, whether it be his manager or whether it be a senior person within a unit. And a very careful monitoring is made of anything that would appear to be . . . gratuitous information or even unrelated information.

Mary Benson and Steven Hunter expected an easy acceptance of their application for an auto loan from Wells Fargo Bank. They had adequate earnings and more than $10,000 deposited in Wells Fargo accounts. Their loan application was denied twice. First, Benson applied by herself. After the first rejection, Hunter added his name to the application. Benson and Hunter then received a letter from Wells Fargo stating that the rejection was due to insufficient credit history. The letter listed TRW and Credit Bureau, Inc., as the principal sources of information. The couple requested to see their files at the credit agencies under the Fair Credit Reporting Act.

Neither bureau listed Benson's Visa account with Wells Fargo or her credit history covering the period she lived in Minnesota. The information in the files contained many errors. Benson checked with Wells Fargo and was told that the loan department had no way of confirming that she had a Visa account with the bank. The assistant manager of Wells Fargo's Installment Loan Application Center stated there was no way for a loan officer to get in-house information on an applicant's credit worthiness. "It does not fit into our procedure. . . . We do not go and direct check our own loans. . . . There is no procedure that we use." Wells Fargo relied on outside credit information, even though it had extensive credit records of its own. Benson's incredulous reaction was, "My impression is that the left hand doesn't know what the right hand is doing, and there's a supreme arrogance that overrules the whole thing."

Tenant-Screening Agencies

An extension of the credit-reporting services is the tenant-screening agency, often operated by subsidiaries of such well-known firms as TRW and Tymshare. This kind of agency is often faced with the same problems as credit-reporting services. Accuracy sometimes is questioned, and items included on reports cannot always be substantiated.

A tenant in Santa Monica, California, for example, was asked to move within thirty days when a new owner took over his building and wanted the apartment. It took more than a month to find a new apartment, and at the end of the thirty days, the owner issued an eviction notice for the record. After the tenant located a new apartment and made a deposit, a tenant-screening service discovered the routine eviction notice and his lease was denied. There was no explanation of the basis for the eviction notice in the records, and the tenant was forced to spend months battling it out with the computer while suffering the indignity of trying to convince a new, skeptical landlord of the facts.

Initiating the Credit Relationship

To obtain credit, one must apply for it and be evaluated according to a credit grantor's criteria of credit worthiness based upon personal information about the applicant. Credit grantors differ with respect to the amount of information they seek, the extent to which they verify and supplement this data, and the factors they use to gauge credit worthiness. These variations are influenced by the technological sophistication of the grantor and its stake in the credit relationship. For example, a credit grantor with a standardized, reliable method of predicting responsible credit use may not need credit bureau reports.

In initiating the credit process, an applicant divulges information about himself to the credit grantor, usually by filling out an application form. The grantor verifies and supplements the answers on the form via inquiry to a credit bureau or some other source such as another credit grantor or the applicant's employer. Credit applications rarely indicate the full extent of the additional inquiries the credit grantor will make.

The need for independent information sources is a common theme of credit grantors. A spokesman for the J. C. Penney Company candidly stated, "Let us not overlook a significant fact. . . . people tend to state their case most favorably when they know that the information they supply will be the basis of their having their application granted. It is essential that we be permitted to verify the information presented to us by the applicant through credit bureaus and others."

In the past, credit application evaluation involved a good deal of judgment in applying general standards of credit worthiness. But today, the mushrooming credit demand is driving many grantors, particularly the larger ones, to experiment with methods that promise to be both less costly and more reliable. One technique, called "point scoring," bases an applicant's credit worthiness on a small cluster of personal characteristics which statistics show to be a reliable measure of ability and willingness to pay. For example, there is statistical evidence that people in some occupations are more likely to repay credit obligations than people in other occupations, and a numerical value can be assigned to the differences.

The same is true of people who own their homes as compared to those who rent. Another factor is how long a person has lived at the same address. Under this system, the applicant is rated according to the number of points he scores on these predictive characteristics. The characteristics in a particular point-scoring cluster and the numerical value assigned to each may vary from one credit grantor to another and by geographic area. Also, a grantor may revise its formula from time to time in response to its experience with customers and changing economic conditions.

One advantage of point scoring is that it may eliminate the need for a credit report. On the other hand, it effectively eliminates the individual's opportunity to challenge the credit decision. Point scoring and other credit policies which predict credit worthiness entirely on group behavior diminish individuality as a factor in granting credit, and could eliminate it entirely. In this area, legal protections do not appear to be keeping pace with credit evaluation practices.

The Equal Credit Opportunity Act, which permits a rejected applicant to request the reasons for an adverse credit decision, relies on the theory that an adverse decision can be explained in terms of one or more characteristics in an overall score. Point scoring, however, submerges particular characteristics in an overall score making it virtually impossible to pinpoint the exact reason for a denial of credit. The Fair Credit Reporting Act, which also permits a rejected applicant to request the reasons for an adverse credit decision, relies on the concept that the decision can be traced to one or more individual characteristics. Since point scoring hides individual characteristics in an overall formularized pattern based on a combination of statistically weighted factors, the credit-granting decision is totally dehumanized, and a change in the weighting of factors could affect the decision.

The Credit Card Society

It is doubtful that any other innovation in the history of consumer credit has had a more profound impact than the credit card. It has transformed the consumer-credit relationship, and a new record-keeping industry has grown up around it. A credit card program cannot operate safely unless the credit grantor can monitor credit card transactions and deny credit when it sees fit.

The type of credit authorization hinges primarily on the size of the card issuer's system. Giant issuers like Sears and American Express operate their own authorization networks. The bank credit card is the fastest growing financial service today, and most banks belong to service organizations that supplement their own systems to provide worldwide coverage. Airlines, hotels, and restaurants often use independent authorization services that provide information obtained from other major card issuers.

At the hub of any authorization system is the distribution of regularly updated listings of accounts that have been cancelled or overextended and cards that have been stolen or lost. The merchant is protected against loss by checking this list before putting through the transaction. The credit issuer guarantees payment for all accounts which are not on the list.

An authorization system also protects the credit grantor by limiting its risk. Where the total amount that may be charged to an account is specified in advance, an overextension is flagged automatically. Where the credit limit is not specified, the system triggers intervention when the balance owed becomes larger than normal. Trained evaluators then review the account to determine if the balance appears to be out of line. Most authorization systems also monitor credit card accounts for unusual activity that might indicate fraud. Techniques are available which immediately provide the card issuer with an up-to-date status report on any card holder's account.

Card issuers disclose negative information to independent authorization services which in turn pass it along to their subscribers on request. Although the independents—airlines, hotels, restaurants, retailers, etc.—operate in many respects like other card issuers, they represent additional arms of the network. Thus, where derogatory information exists, it is doubtful that the individual knows it exists or in how many files it appears. If he does learn he was rejected by a specific credit grantor because of inaccurate or outdated information in his record, he has no way of knowing in how many other places the same information appears.

Your Legal Rights

You owe it to yourself to know your rights, limited though they may be, and then to exercise those rights in order to minimize injury to your personal reputation or opportunities. Where adverse credit, financial, character, or life-style information appears against you in a consumer credit file, you have a right to learn its nature and substance, its accuracy, and to challenge and learn the source of the information. Adverse information about you that is more than seven years old should be purged from your file. The main sources of consumer protection in credit relationships are three federal statutes: the Fair Credit Reporting Act (FCRA); the Fair Credit Billing Act (FCBA); and the Equal Credit Opportunity Act.

The FCRA essentially gives consumers the right to know the nature, substance, and sources of information maintained by a consumer reporting agency. If you have been denied credit, the credit grantor is required to disclose the nature of the information upon which an adverse decision was based. If the denial was wholly or partly because of information contained in a report from a consumer reporting agency, the creditor must supply the name and address of the reporting agency.

Upon receipt of a written request, the reporting agency must disclose to you the nature and substance of all information (except medical information) it has on you. Some credit bureaus will send you a copy of your report. Credit bureaus must also disclose the sources of their information and all recent recipients of the report.

If you find mistakes in your credit report, the credit bureau will reinvestigate the item and eliminate it if it cannot be confirmed. Pay particular attention to the dates corresponding with adverse items of information contained in the report. It has been demonstrated that several credit agencies' policies encourage the compilation of adverse information. However, the FCRA, with very limited exceptions, prohibits the reporting of adverse information which is more than seven years old. If you are still not satisfied, provide the company with a statement of less than one hundred words which will be included in your report. At your request, your side of the dispute will be sent to anyone who received your original report.

A deficiency of the FCRA is its failure to assure the correction of adverse information erroneously disclosed by a credit grantor to a credit-reporting bureau. Although federal law does provide individuals with the right to correct adverse information held about them, the correction process is not easy. In fact, it so angered Jack Stone that he resolved to make purchases on a cash basis. With a good income, he applied to his bank for a premium service it offered. As part of the application process, he had to submit a personal financial statement. The bank sent him a form letter rejecting his application on the basis of a report from the credit bureau. At the credit-reporting agency, he examined the twelve items on his report, each of which had an error. He wrote a letter to the company explaining all the errors. He then contacted the companies listed on his report to have them request corrected reports from the bureau so he could forward a new credit report to his bank. Finally, after weeks of effort, his file was corrected and his record cleared.

Under the FCRA, however, you cannot sue for an invasion of privacy, defamation of character, or negligence if you have suffered on account of a false credit report. This immunity extends to credit bureaus, consumer investigative agencies, and to those who provide the information about you in the first place. Nevertheless, as a spokesperson for the Associated Credit Bureaus, Inc., pointed out, while the FCRA may not specifically provide the basis for such a suit, individuals were not prohibited from suing credit bureaus, consumer investigative agencies, or those providing information to these firms.

Some of the thirteen states that have enacted legislation based on the FCRA, including California, Maine, and New York, have deleted this immunity from their laws. Also, in Maine and New York credit-reporting companies must be authorized by the consumer before furnishing a report.

The FCRA is supplemented by the Fair Credit Billing Act (FCBA). If you wish to dispute a bill, promptly contact the credit grantor in writing. In the letter, provide your name and account number, the dollar amount of the suspected error, and, if possible, a brief explanation of the error.

The credit grantor must acknowledge receipt of the letter unless the error has already been corrected. Within ninety days, it must either correct the error or explain why it believes the bill was correct. After receipt of your letter, the credit grantor cannot try to collect any amount questioned, nor can it report you to others as delinquent. However, the amount in dispute can be applied against your credit limit.

The Equal Credit Opportunity Act prohibits discrimination in the granting of credit based on race, national origin, sex, marital status, welfare payments, or age (unless you are not old enough to enter into a binding contract). Married persons may have credit information listed in the husband's and wife's names separately, and creditors may see only the file of the spouse who applied for credit.

In response to "abundant evidence of the use of abusive, deceptive, and unfair debt collection practices by many debt collectors contributing to the number of personal bankruptcies, marital instability, the loss of jobs, and invasions of personal privacy," Congress created the Fair Debt Collection Practices Act in 1978. Debt collectors are prohibited from using any false, deceptive, or misleading representations in connection with the collection of the debt, nor may they engage in any harassing, oppressive, or abusive behavior such as threats of violence or profane language. Debt collectors must communicate with consumers during convenient hours and may only engage in limited communication with third parties. Debt collectors who fail to comply with any of the provisions of the act may be held liable for actual and punitive damages. The act was strengthened by an amendment in 1986 that added new restrictions for debt-collecting lawyers. Attorneys had been exempted from coverage by the 1978 law when acting on behalf of their clients. The Debt Collection Act of 1982 further outlines actions which may be taken by the government concerning indebtedness to the United States.

If any aspect of your credit relationship falls short of the requirements outlined above, your rights may have been violated. Do not be discouraged by a lack of state or local legislation concerning these issues in your area. These rights are protected by federal law. Contact your local state's attorney to see if your rights have been violated.

Conclusion

Individual credit information is collected and circulated by consumer reporting bureaus and commercial credit grantors on a large scale. Methods used for the collection of personal data are not always conducive to accuracy, and often the reports are circulated to a wide variety of users before mistakes can be detected, if at all. Credit reports that contain inaccurate information due to human error or careless investigative methods can have disturbing results for the subjects. Although erroneous reports may be challenged, it is not always possible to fully make corrections.

It is important to know the rights afforded individuals by existing federal statutes. The customer has the right to know on what basis credit is denied and the name of the company that produced the adverse report. This information is essential if an erroneous report is to be corrected. Data on an individual that is questioned in a credit bureau report has to be reinvestigated, and unconfirmed data eliminated. The consumer also has the right to place a short rebuttal in the report, and he should request that it be sent to recipients of the original report. Adverse material must be deleted after a period of seven years.

The rights provided by law, limited though they may be, are for your protection. Individuals should check their personal credit reports, know their rights under the law, and be ready to challenge errors.

10

Do You Know Where Your Name, Address, and Profile Are?

Society is continually pushing in on the individual. He has only a few areas in which he can be himself, free from external restraint or observation.

—Edward Vaughan Long

Following a visit to her doctor's office, a young wife learned she was pregnant. Immediately thereafter the expectant mother was deluged with mail from suppliers of items ranging from diaper service and baby carriages to insurance and furniture. Since she had not informed anyone of her condition, she assumed it was released by her doctor and accused him of breaching the confidential relationship between physician and patient. On investigation it was revealed that while in the doctor's waiting room, she had filled out a card offering free literature on prenatal and postnatal hygiene, thereby unwittingly placing her name on a list compiler's mailing list. It was through the rash of mail solicitations, including a jumbo postcard for a diaper service that announced in large print, "CONGRATULATIONS NEW MOTHER. We want you to know that as soon as the new baby arrives, we are prepared to furnish you with the best diaper service in the nation," that her family learned of her pregnancy, a fact she was not ready to disclose.

Without your knowledge, you are profiled and placed on many lists, whether you like it or not. These lists are used for marketing solicitations as well as many other purposes, often affecting how others interact with you. Do you know what gets you on which lists, or some of the ways the lists are used?

It is much easier to get on many mailing lists than to stay off. In fact, to stay off, you would have to live like a hermit on a deserted island. Typically, your name gets on a mailing list:

• By merely *being*—living at a particular address, subscribing to telephone service, voting in an election, registering for just about anything whether you are compelled to by law or not.

• By functioning like a human—getting your name in the paper, getting married or divorced, having a baby, going to school, getting a job or in some cases losing one, relocating to a new home or apartment, joining a social or religious group, or buying an automobile.

• By responding to mail solicitation—not only does this get you on mailing lists, it makes you a favored prospect. It tells sellers of products, services, candidates, or causes that you are a likely candidate for buying what they have to offer through the mail.

Selectivity: The Key Factor

The average person is unaware of the automatic follow-up to such seemingly small and innocuous action as subscribing to a magazine, a move that will probably result in about twenty-five additional solicitations within the year. It is also highly probable that the type of magazine you subscribe to, book you buy, or organization you join or contribute to will be entered into a data bank to be matched with other publicly or privately available information about you that will round out your profile or record. This will help the computer to scan characteristics required for specific purposes, and thus automatically and at mind-boggling speeds identify people who are most apt to respond favorably to solicitations for vacations abroad, gambling junkets, home refurbishing, education or cultural opportunities, women's liberation, anti-abortion legislation, or liberal or conservative causes and candidates. When it comes to direct-mail merchandising, the key factor is selectivity.

With the cost of mail advertising campaigns moving steadily upward, no mailer can afford to waste labor, postage, or computer time on people who probably would not even consider the offer being made. What today's knowledgeable marketer looks for most of all is a predictable chance of an affirmative response, and the best gauge of this is affirmative action in the past. Thus, the "hottest" list a marketer could rent is of buyers, subscribers, donors, or voters who already are on record as having bought, subscribed, donated, or voted the way he wants, and preferably not too long ago. That is why the best list an organization could use is its own list of customers and prospects.

People who take time out to answer "no" to a direct-mail solicitation are very likely to be put on other mailing lists because they are considered to be among the most responsive to direct mail campaigns.

For example, the American Museum of Natural History made plans to offer for rent 200,000 names and addresses of persons who responded "no" to a membership offer. These people are considered good prospects for collectibles, charities, gourmet food and wine, books, audio cassettes, or just about any-thing that has to do with the American Museum of Natural History. Publishers Central Bureau rents the "no" responses it receives from sweepstakes entries to insurance companies, other contest merchandisers, mail-order real estate firms, and publishers of self-improvement materials.

Presorted Mail

The U.S. Postal Service classifies all unsolicited mail as third class, which over the last ten years has been by far the largest-growing mail category. The *Annual Report of the Postmaster General* (1986) and the *Comprehensive Statement of Postal Operations* (1986), convey some interesting statistics. Nearly 37 billion pieces were delivered in 1982. By 1986, that figure had risen to 55 billion, nearly a 49 percent increase. The largest increase occurred for mail presorted to a carrier route, which reached a volume of 24.6 billion pieces. Third-class mail is expected to increase 10 percent a year.

A presorted service for the nation's direct mailers has been available since the late seventies. This service, which currently lowers unit costs to 10.1 cents, is the main factor behind the recent explosion in volume of third-class mail. But another important reason is the pervasiveness of mailing lists, and the fact that direct-mail advertising is the major marketing tool of many enterprises. Also contributing to this growth has been the increase of shared mailings. In such arrangements, preprinted advertising circulars of several merchants are combined in a single third-class mailing, frequently accom-panied by a detached address label presorted to a carrier route. Whatever the cause, the U.S. Postal Service is relying to a greater and greater extent on the revenue generated by this means. In 1986, third-class mail revenue was $5.6 billion. Total Post Office revenue for the year was $30 billion.

Mailing-List Compilers

While some mailers jealously guard their own lists and deny others access to them, others encourage rental and exchange because they want to expand the number of individuals who are likely to take responsive action to solicitations by mail. According to a spokesperson for Time, Inc., it is good business for *Time* magazine to make its lists available to other direct mailers. One result is "to enlarge the universe of active mail-order buyers. Our experience shows that the more one has purchased by mail in the past the most likely he is to appreciate the real value and the convenience of doing business by mail."

Because a business may be "sitting on a gold mine" and not even know it, Ed Burnett Consultants, Inc., offers a list management service. They suggest that businesses market their customer lists to receive rental income. In his capacity as list manager, Ed Burnett promotes the sale and rental of lists, reviews and approves prospective customers' sample mailing pieces, processes list orders, and collects fees. Burnett's firm manages such diverse lists as the National Association of Female Executives' membership roster, *Football News*'s active subscribers, and Pioneer Stereo component buyers.

It is interesting to note that the Chesapeake and Potomac Telephone Company reversed an announced decision to rent customer lists estimated to bring in $300,000 a year due to the overwhelmingly negative response from its Virginia customers. The company intends to continue with the rental plan in the District of Columbia and Maryland. The plan will exclude only those customers with unlisted numbers and those who choose not to participate.

The Twin Foundation, a firm located in Providence, Rhode Island, currently has about 20,000 twins listed in its Twin Registry data base. The foundation provides information on twins to scientists, parents, and other interested individuals from its computerized information bank and research library.

Narrowing down the population to its likely prospects is big business today, and a big-volume business at that. The president of Publishers' Clearing House stated his firm "predominantly sells magazine subscriptions by mail and we do it by sending mailing pieces to our own past customers and to people on other lists that we rent through the normal list rental procedure. The mailings are very large-scale. . . . The outside lists that we get are predominantly lists of people who have taken a mail-order action. We find that they are very much more productive for us and that is of course the name of the game. That produces the most orders." In 1985, Publishers' Clearing House reached around 75 percent of all households in the United States, according to its chairman, William Renert.

Most direct-mail campaigns that draw better than a 2 percent positive response are regarded as successful. The total sales volume of all direct marketing and related service industries now approaches $150 billion. The Direct Marketing Association (DMA) now consists of about 3,500 firms in this country and abroad, representing all kinds of industries. All of them market goods and services through direct response methods, including direct-mail advertising and mailing lists. As an advertising outlet, it stands third behind newspapers and television, and draws about twice as many advertising dollars as either radio or magazines. The industry obviously is critical to the nation's economy.

The names on the mailing lists can originate from almost anywhere, including such sources as public records, telephone directories, and government registries. State and local government agencies compile records on such things as the year, make, and model of registered automobiles at a given address, holders of hunting or fishing licenses, property owners, and registered voters.

Ed Burnett Consultants, Inc., indicates that it employs a full-time librarian to supervise its list library which "includes over 1,000 current sources, plus over 4,200 alphabetic and classified phone directories . . . ordered annually month by month, via computer." The main sources of information used in compiling the firm's lists are directories, rosters, registrations, membership rolls, former members, newspapers, phone books, credit references, and government reports.

Donnelley Marketing, a major public-record compiler, holds information on 79 million households (90 percent of those in the United States) in its Donnelley Quality Index (DQI) files.

The company's literature states:

> The specific DQI2 gives the innovative direct marketer insight into—and access to—over 79 million unduplicated households. It is the only consumer database compiled from telephone directories and auto registration information (from R. L. Polk). . . . The DQI2 goes beyond geographic area selectivity. Each residential unit in the database is identified as an individual family structure. The basic DQI database is enriched annually with outside list sources verifying sex, age, presence of children, mail responsiveness, and lifestyle interests. Where a database record matches one or more of the external files—for example, each one with age and sex information—the data is recorded for the respective household. In households where the data is incomplete, sophisticated modeling techniques . . . are used to complete the picture. Input data for these techniques included individual household characteristics, census area statistics, the Target Finder Marketing Information System, and Cluster Plus.

Each household is scored on the computer record according to the probability that its members will respond in each of the designated marketing areas. For each area, Donnelley can provide a highly sophisticated profile of various geographic locations to enable marketers to plan promotions and target the most likely households.

Richard A. Viguerie, who heads a multiple-response compiling firm that handles both political fund-raising solicitations and subscription campaigns slanted at people with conservative political views, described to the USPPC his handling of the names in his master file: "If it is a name that has responded to a mailing, we have the month and the year that they responded. And, of course, their name and address and ZIP code. We have the amount of their contribution, and many times, we have the source of where the name came from. In other words, if we rented a magazine list of businessmen, we have a notation that this is a person who is a businessman, so that he is going to be interested in subscribing to business publications perhaps or some such as that."

From rather modest beginnings, the number of names in Viguerie's "master file" rose dramatically to reach a peak in 1980 with the massive mailing effort that accompanied the election of President Reagan. In 1984, Viguerie sent out around 102 million pieces of mail. The company's master file is now reported to contain 4.5 million names, and is rented by an estimated thirty-five conservative groups. The method of formulation has essentially remained the same since the company was started. Sources of names include magazine subscribers, purchasers of selected products, contributors to campaigns and causes, people who answer surveys, and others who get on lists because they are who they are. The company also makes increasing use of the DMA mail preference tapes through which they are able to update their master file around ten times a year. "Really, we've got to the point where we have just about all the information we need," says Walter Longyear, vice president of the Viguerie Company.

Information of this kind is obtained from the return card or order form which is coded with the desired identification characteristics. The coded information is then picked up by the computer in large operations. If a person does not respond to a magazine ad for a correspondence course, his name will not get into the file. If he does, however, he will be on record as having bought the course or as subscribing to the particular magazine. Given the speeds and economies of electronic data processing, this concept can be carried to imaginative extremes so that, assuming the appropriate promotional requirement, a mailer's solicitation could be limited to those who are pro-Star Wars defense, who contributed money to the Pat Robertson election campaign, belong to the National Rifle Association, and subscribe to *Barron's* or *Forbes*. This could tell much about a person's buying and voting proclivities.

David Cohen, former president of Common Cause, points out, "Political candidates in order to meet the matching requirements of the Federal Election Campaign Act must reach substantial numbers of individuals to solicit mail contributions. Direct mail is a principal means of doing this. National public interest groups concerned with issues also are heavily dependent on direct mail to get their messages to individuals who are interested in responding. And, in both cases, direct mail affords interested individuals an opportunity to participate."

"Certainly Common Cause could not have mobilized 200,000 citizens within its first year and sustained a membership level of close to 300,000 in subsequent years without access to the mails through mailing lists secured by exchange or rental. Seventy-five percent of all our new members come to us through response to unsolicited mail," says Kathy Covall, Director of Fund Raising for Common Cause. According to Covall, Common Cause has a 70 percent renewal rate of membership. Each year 30 percent of new members have to be recruited, and therefore the organization is very dependent on unsolicited mailings for this purpose.

Mailing-list compilers' catalogs listing the various profiled groups available for rental run as large as an inch and a half thick. They include such catagories as foreign-policy hawks, people who frequent the dice tables, and affluent ethnic professionals. You may also designate the kind of person in the country you would like to identify, and list compilers will develop such a list on order. The names and addresses are then rented to subscribers for about 3 1/2 cents per name.

Some extremist organizations have set themselves up to identify Americans who, in their judgment, are undesirable, such as persons who are "race traitors" and "enemies." These lists are made available to subscribers.

You don't know what lists you are on, or how a particular list may be used. Some lists may be used to deny you a job or promotion, a government appointment, credit, or admission to a club or school.

On 25 June 1985, I received a letter from John C. Sutphen, Senior Vice President for Consumer Card Marketing of American Express, as follows:

Dear Mr. Linowes:
Your good name. . .your fine reputation. . .your standing among your friends and in your community. . .are the rewards of a lifetime of responsibility.
Another is the Gold Card. And because of your excellent credentials, you have been accepted for Gold Card Membership on a *pre-approved* basis, so obtaining the Gold Card couldn't be easier.

Five and one-half pages of single-spaced type later, it closed with the P.S.: "It takes credentials to get credentials. And acquiring the Gold Card is no exception. I am pleased to be able to enclose the short Pre-approved Enrollment Form, since your credentials already speak for you."

What credentials? How did Mr. Sutphen know about my reputation or standing among my friends or in the community? I never met the man.

Here's how the system works, according to a 13 June 1985 letter from P. Sliman, a Bank of America official: The bank uses a well-recognized and legally approved process known as "prescreening." With prescreening, a list of names is created by using one of the following methods:

1. The bank purchases or rents a list of names aimed at a certain market segment from national list brokers who compile these names from a number of sources. The list is then sent to a credit bureau which is asked to check a limited number of pieces of information in its records to determine whether the names on the list meet certain credit criteria provided by the bank.

2. The bank sends its credit criteria to a credit bureau. The credit bureau is then asked to create a list of names from its own files based upon the bank's credit criteria.

Once the list of prescreened names is created by the credit bureau, it is *not* returned directly to the bank. Rather, it is sent to a company specializing in mailing (usually a data-processing house). The third party then mails the offers directly to the eligible candidates. The only time the bank learns the identities of the recipients is when those individuals voluntarily choose to respond to the mailing.

Prescreening

For marketing purposes, pinpointing potentially favorable respondents is only part of the selection procedure in some cases. Under certain circumstances, it becomes useful to weed out of existing lists people who, because they have poor credit records, are undesirable prospects. In this type of "prescreening" selection where a credit bureau's files are used, names are dropped from lists.

Occasionally solicitations cause unexpected reactions. One day Bruce Steinberg received an unsolicited form letter from the Bank of America asking him to join the 33 million people already using a BankAmericard. The letter cited Steinberg's "excellent credit reputation." Steinberg decided to investigate the source of the claim, leading him to sue TRW Credit Data. He said TRW had not asked his permission to give out his name, and that the company had not informed him of their action when he made a specific request under the Fair Credit Reporting Act. Steinberg eventually settled out of court for more than $35,000 (including legal fees) and an agreement by TRW to change their prescreening procedures.

The direct-marketing industry views mailing lists as a form of communication protected by the First Amendment. Others contend that the only possible way to control a gigantic industry's abuses of information they get for nothing is to legislate against it. Where government lists are concerned, they argue the individual has no choice at all but to be on the list, which points up an even greater need to control lists maintained by government agencies.

As referred to in Chapter 6, the Internal Revenue Service has been studying the feasibility of using commercial mailing lists to identify non-filers of tax returns. In December 1983, the IRS obtained a commercial list file containing 1982 data on about two million households with an estimated annual income of $10,000 or more. The data were then matched with IRS records to identify potential non-filers.

In testimony before the Senate Subcommittee on Oversight of Government Management in June 1984, Roscoe L. Egger, Jr., then commissioner of the Internal Revenue Service, admitted that "we do not know the specific sources of the data in the commercial list we received." The then chairman of the Direct Marketing Association stated at the same hearings: "We have serious reservations about their use of any mailing lists, whether they are compiled from public or private sources."

The IRS action contradicts a DMA guideline that lists should be rented for marketing purposes only. Hence, most commercial mailing list firms have refused to rent their lists to the IRS. The DMA chairman explained the critical distinction: "I think the public understands perfectly well from their experience up to now, all that happens as the result of being on a mailing list is that you get mail. You read it or you throw it away. And that is essentially a benign process. But if the public ever comes to feel personal privacy is endangered by this process, they could change their attitude entirely. . . . With that in mind, the business community has done what we think is an effective job in seeing to it that consumer privacy is maintained. We believe the IRS has an obligation to do the same."

What About Government Lists?

One of the searching questions we have to face asks if it is proper for a government agency to make the lists it maintains available for commercial use or to private individuals.

Advocates of regulation for the mailing-list industry are particularly disturbed that the inclusion of a person's name on various government agency lists as a result of having to register a motor vehicle or gun, voting, or responding to a census survey often means his name will be added to commercial mailing lists as well. They maintain that an individual should have the option to deny such use.

The rules affecting the mailing-list practices of government agencies are murky. At the federal level, some lists must be made available, the disclosure of some is prohibited, and the availability of others is uncertain.

It was thought that the Privacy Act of 1974 would have some impact on the availability of federal records and lists that could be used for commercial mailing purposes. While it has had a modest effect in some agencies, there are major conflicts of interest. One major conflict is with the Freedom of Information Act (FOIA) which operates on a presumption of disclosure unless there are compelling reasons to the contrary. One such exception is the so-called b(6) exemption—forbidding release if there is a "clearly unwarranted invasion of privacy." Do mailing lists of names and addresses constitute such a threat? The answer is by no means clear.

Take the Drug Enforcement Agency (DEA), for example. This agency handles a large amount of information on medical practitioners and other registered handlers of controlled substances. For the purpose of public access law, such individuals are considered to be businesses. Hence the names and addresses of such handlers can be given out as a matter of course, without invading the privacy of the handler, or invoking the b(6) exemption. Registration numbers can be given out if the person making the request has a DEA registration number. John Means, Freedom of Information Act and Privacy Coordinator of DEA, told my research assistant in a November 1987 interview that lists of registered handlers are given out in this way regularly to drug distributors, wholesalers, and other people in the medical field. For a small fee, the computer tape is released. According to Means, "There's no way we can deny that information. We consider them as businesses." He adds, however, that there has been no noticeable abuse of this right and little controversy.

In other federal departments, however, stricter protections for mailing lists do apply. The Department of the Interior, for example, does not disclose its mailing lists as a matter of policy, even with a FOIA request. The Veterans Administration, too, having a store of potentially useful names and addresses of former servicemen, has a firm policy of nondisclosure. The only exceptions to this rule are the releases to certain governmental and non-profit organizations for the checking of benefit eligibility, health and safety purposes, and for debt collection.

However, the overall position of federal agencies with regard to disclosure is ambiguous, and several court cases have failed to clarify the standards and interests involved. Consequently, agencies make lists of project directors, business executives, college presidents, and other individuals available at cost to anyone who asks for them, and the names of people who ask to be included on a specific government agency mailing list may be added to other lists as well.

At the state level, several states now restrict in some way the use of motor vehicle registration information for commercial mailing purposes. Restrictions are usually included in motor vehicle department regulations or in contracts with list compilers who may be permitted to use the information for statistical, but not commercial purposes.

R. L. Polk, a direct-marketing firm which gets its lists mainly from automobile registries, mails motor vehicle recall notifications to car owners. Irving Ray, Assistant Research Director for Polk, said that his company now is restricted by some state privacy laws from using those lists for mailing purposes. Other states regard such information as motor vehicle registry, mortgages, and various types of licensing as public records which are made available to list compilers for whatever purposes they wish. On a nationwide basis, very little consistency exists.

In Los Angeles, a superior court judge ruled that Californians have a right to sue for damages if credit card companies sell their names and addresses for other companies' mailing lists. In Indiana, state agencies are prohibited from providing commercial or charitable solicitors with their mailing lists unless specifically authorized to do so.

In 1983, the state of New York became the tenth state to enact a personal privacy protection law. New York's law gives individuals the right to correct records they believe to be inaccurate; establishes guidelines for the gathering, retention, and release of information on individuals; and requires a review by the Committee on Open Government before an agency could begin a computer-match program. The act also tries to limit the disclosure of citizens' records. A 1981 study showed that 48 percent of the data collected by New York state agencies had been released to other agencies and individuals. Governor Mario Cuomo strongly supported the measure, saying, "In accepting the benefits provided by these new technologies, government must also accept responsibility for their intelligent use."

The state of Minnesota is in a somewhat peculiar position with regard to mailing lists. Minnesota's public access statute is the most liberal in the country, requiring a disclosure of information unless the legislature has specifically legislated an exception. This provides an open door for the release of lists of names from official public records, and state lists are now used for an increasingly wide variety of commercial and private purposes. According to Donald Gemberling, Director of Minnesota's Data Privacy Division, in an interview with my assistant in June 1988, list sales bring the state about $3 million in revenue each year. There is no privacy exemption in the public access law, and very little pressure to reform a practice that brings in that amount of revenue. Gemberling stated, "What little opposition there is to the practice is overwhelmed by the revenue that list sales bring in."

In Massachusetts, virtually everything touched by a government bureaucrat may be released to the public upon request pursuant to the state's Freedom of Information Act. In a 18 July 1985 discussion of the act, the *Boston Globe* illustrated the startling amount of personal information that could be obtained under state law:

> Anyone could go to public records and find that Joseph Brown (not a real name) is 58 years old and married to a woman named Mary, works as an engineer, drives a Cadillac, owns a motor boat, holds a hunting license and a fresh water fishing license, and is an officer in a corporation.
>
> The same public record will show that his wife, Mary, is a 56-year-old physical therapist who drives a Chevrolet.
>
> Their 30-year-old son, David Brown, lives in Boston in a condominium with a mortgage rate of 13.5 percent. He works as an accountant, owns a snowmobile, drives a Volvo, and donated money to the 1984 campaign of Governor Dukakis.
>
> All of that information is available for free or a minimal reproduction charge from the Bureau of Vital Statistics, the Division of Registration, the Registry of Motor Vehicles, the Division of Fisheries and Wildlife, the Division of Marine Recreational Vehicles, the Corporation Division of the Secretary of State's Office, the Registry of Deeds, and the Office of Campaign and Political Finance.

Under certain circumstances, individuals may feel they suffer tangible damage because of their appearance on mailing lists. In one publicized case, a doctor, after registering his gun collection with the Bureau of Alcohol, Tobacco, and Firearms as required by law, found himself inundated with sales literature from gun dealers. Apart from the annoyance, what concerned him most was that with his name accessible on such a list, he believed he was being set up as a target for burglary. As a result of his anxiety, he insured his gun collection and installed a burglar alarm system in his home at considerable expense. Some argue that individuals listed as rare coin or stamp collectors are equally vulnerable.

An established security company sent a form letter to 5,000 people they believed to be art, gem, or coin collectors. In the letter, the company pointed out how vulnerable those people were to criminals who could buy the same list of names and that the people needed that company's system to protect themselves. The director of technical practices at the Direct Marketing Association commented about the use of this kind of targeted mailing list, saying, "It is lacking in taste, borders on being unethical, and impinges on the consumer's privacy." DMA has issued a series of guidelines on personal information protection and has established the Ethical Business Practice Committee to implement them, even though the organization has no policing power.

Article 31 of DMA's ethical guidelines states that "All list owners, brokers, managers, compilers, and users should be protective of the consumer's right to privacy and sensitive to the information collected on lists and subsequently considered for transfer, rental, sale, or exchange. Information such as, but not limited to, medical, financial, insurance or court data, and data that may be considered to be personal and intimate in nature by all reasonable standards should not be included on lists that are made available for transfer, rental, sale or exchange when there is a reasonable expectation by the consumer that the information would be kept confidential."

Article 33 proscribes the use of any list or list data, ". . . in violation of the lawful rights of the list owner or of the agreement between the parties; any such misuse should be brought to the attention of the lawful owner."

The DMA's ethical guidelines also describe appropriate techniques to be used in telephone marketing. The following suggestions are made in Articles 34 through 38:

All telephone contacts should be made during reasonable hours.

At no time should "high pressure" tactics be utilized.

No telephone marketer should solicit sales using automatic electronic dialing equipment unless the telephone immediately disconnects when the called person hangs up.

Taping of telephone conversations should not be conducted without all-party consent or the use of a beeping device.

Telephone marketers should remove the name of any contact from their telephone lists when requested to do so.

Telephone marketers should not call telephone subscribers who have unlisted or unpublished telephone numbers unless a prior relationship exists.

Getting Off Mailing Lists

A convincing argument against government regulation of mailing list marketing is that one has the option of discarding an unsolicited letter of advertisement without opening it. Despite the annoyance they cause some people, selected unsolicited mailings can be beneficial to society, and if you receive unsolicited merchandise through the mail, you have the option of either throwing it away or keeping it without paying for it.

For those who wish to have their names removed from mailing lists, the Direct Marketing Association has designed its Mail Preference Service (MPS). Under this system, if Mr. Jones wants less unsolicited mail, he can write to the DMA requesting that his name and address be removed. This information is then placed on a computer tape and circulated to the various business subscribers of MPS who act as service bureaus for the great majority of the nation's direct mailers. Since its inception in 1971, about 725,000 consumers have asked to have their names removed. These names are kept on file for five years and then updated.

An increasing number of businesses are complying with the DMA's ethical guideline stating that "Every list owner who sells, exchanges, or rents lists should see to it that each individual on the list is informed of those practices, and should offer an option to have the individual's name deleted when rentals or purchases are made."

Illinois Bell informed its customers of its policy concerning this issue in "An Important Notice About Mailing Lists We Supply To Others," a company mailing:

Direct marketers have asked to rent our customer lists in order to contact you with sales information.

We believe this would provide you with a useful service. At the same time, the revenues we receive from this activity can be used to help hold down the overall price of the telephone service.

Many people want to receive sales information from direct marketers. It helps them find the best bargains on items they want to buy.

However, if you would rather not receive such advertising, please fill in this form and return it to us. We will then remove your name from the list we supply to direct marketers. This action will not affect your directory listing, nor will it prevent direct marketers from using information that is in published directories. (If you have a non-published or non-listed number, you need not respond; your name is automatically excluded from this list.) You will still receive mailings from Illinois Bell.

This notification and the DMA's guidelines are consistent with recommendations of the U.S. Privacy Protection Commission that an individual should have a way to prevent information about him ostensibly collected for one purpose from being used for another purpose to which he objects.

The DMA used to run an "add-on" service in addition to this "delete service." From 1974 to 1984 about half a million people requested to have their names added to mailing lists. This proved to be too cumbersome a procedure, so they no longer maintain a list of people who want to get more mail. Instead they provide a brochure of relevant direct mail companies to those who inquire. In 1985, DMA began a Telephone Preference Service (TPS) allowing individuals and households to stop the receipt of unsolicited telephone calls. Since 1985, over 150,000 individuals have requested that their names be included in the TPS.

Notes a New Jersey man, "I get a psychological lift from the mail I receive, unsolicited or not. Perhaps the fact that I receive little business mail other than bills, and even less letters from relatives and friends, has something to do with it. But I look forward to reading my mail, and if a particular letter annoys me, I derive a satisfaction out of tossing it unopened into the waste basket knowing that it cost the mailer a quarter or so for the privilege of this treatment at my hands."

Nevertheless, the question still remains, How do you restrain the use of lists for such abusive purposes as unfairly characterizing a person, yet allow constructive uses such as offering the public wanted merchandise? We do not yet have an adequate answer.

The Legal Situation

Prohibitions on the use of mailing lists are limited and inconsistent. The most stringent federal laws relate to the mailing of pornographic materials. Filling out Form 2201 at your local post office serves to notify mailers of such materials to remove your name from their lists. Failure to comply constitutes a federal felony with strict criminal penalties. An individual can get a court order forbidding a mailer to send him such material. The Post Office also maintains a list of individuals who do not wish to receive sexually oriented advertisements. This list is circulated to publishers.

The Privacy Act of 1974 prohibits federal agencies from selling or renting an individual's name and address unless specifically authorized to do so by law. As mentioned earlier, in conflict with this provision, however, is the

Freedom of Information Act which requires disclosure unless there is a "clearly unwarranted invasion of privacy." There is some confusion about whether government mailing lists constitute such a threat. Names and addresses are sometimes not considered to be private information and can be accessible under the FOIA. Because many lists of individuals can be construed as businesses, the departments of Health and Human Services, Education, and Commerce do release lists with business addresses. The Federal Aviation Administration makes available lists of pilots, engineers, navigators, and control tower operators; the Nuclear Regulatory Commission gives the public access to license applications; and the General Services Administration identifies persons who request the purchase of commemorative silver dollars.

The Federal Election Campaign Act requires political candidates for federal office to record your name and address upon receipt of any contribution of $50 or more, and your occupation and principal place of business for contributions exceeding $100. While this information is available for public inspection, the law prohibits its use for political fund-raising or commercial uses.

While in general federal agencies are not to sell or rent mailing lists unless authorized by law or obligated to release them under the Freedom of Information Act, there are very few limits on the disclosure of lists computed by state governments. Minnesota and Washington prohibit the use of voter registration lists for commercial purposes. Florida state law requires that state agencies update their mailing lists and delete obsolete information every two years. Nevada authorizes the state to charge for lists, but prohibits their use for selling products or services. Arizona law merely states that voter registration lists shall be furnished to any person for two cents per name.

Alaska, California, Florida, Illinois, Maryland, Michigan, Nebraska, North Carolina, and Wisconsin prohibit the use of automated dialing equipment to solicit sales or request survey information without the consent of the person called or if not used in conjunction with a live operator. Three states require that such automatic dialing devices disengage immediately when the party called replaces the receiver.

Conclusion

Categorizing individuals has become big business. The compilation of data based on an individual's personal life-style gives marketers a profile of that person's interests and activities. It is virtually impossible to avoid being placed on a mailing list. Specific lists are leased or sold to businesses, politicians, and others who wish to reach a particular group of individuals. This marketing technique not only is cost- and time-effective, but it enables the solicitor to reach those most likely to respond favorably.

Lists are compiled from a wide variety of sources, including magazine subscriptions, book publishers, organizational membership lists, governmental offices, and mail order companies. The various data are combined in pre-determined configurations identifying specific audiences. You may be denied credit, membership, a job, or housing due to an improperly developed list. Not all lists are used in a benign manner. The Freedom of Information Act, the Privacy Act of 1974, and a few other federal statutes give some protection to the individual, but they are not adequate. Some states have enacted privacy measures, but far too many states have inadequate safeguards or none at all. More protection is needed.

11

The Private Investigator: How and Why He Does His Job on You

Private detectives are tapping wires, and are invading the privacy of homes under existing law and nothing is done about it.

—*John L. McClellan*

While engaged on an assignment to unravel the finances of a former utility company employee involved in a $26 million wine-importing fraud exposed by the Securities and Exchange Commission, Virginia private investigator Nick Beltrante got the subject's personnel file from a source in the utility. He then contacted some of his own sources in banks and discovered that the subject had several checking accounts and a few outstanding loans. Using information that had been disclosed to obtain the loans, Beltrante learned that the man owned securities worth about $100,000. A broker friend then helped him get the name of the subject's broker, who confirmed that he had a secret Swiss account.

Beltrante used a contact who was formerly in the Italian national police force who, for a fee, was able to obtain the subject's Swiss bank account number and its balance. This Italian source got around Switzerland's strict banking laws through working contacts made while he was the liaison between the Italian national police and Swiss banking officials. The Italian source learned the Swiss account had about $2 million.

Beltrante said he has many powerful friends in high places, but that he does not make them available to anybody who wants to pay his fee. "I generally want to know the background and reason for every investigation," he said. "I want to do work for good sources. . . . I am certain that my phone has been tapped by government agencies and that I have been investigated over the years."

"I do have sources in the various state and federal enforcement agencies who are willing to exchange data with me on a regular basis. I do not consider these sources as 'illegal sources,'" Beltrante wrote in a letter to me on 7 May 1985. "As a long-time respected professional in my field, *I do not intentionally, or willingly, break the law*. In connection with my sources in public law enforcement, as a private investigator I have volunteered a wealth of valuable data to local, state, and federal enforcement agencies in past years. It has been a long-standing practice for such agencies' representatives to reciprocate and cooperate with 'certain' private investigators.

"Lastly, in connection with congressional sources, I frequently call upon such contacts to obtain data that is normally available to them from IRS, DOD, and CIA, among others. While I know these members of Congress and their aides personally, my requests are always formal, written requests. To date, I have received excellent cooperation from these sources."

With financial investigations now accounting for more than 25 percent of his firm's cases, Beltrante finds that he must often rely on sources within the banking industry to obtain needed financial data. These "information brokers" include computer hackers and bank employees. "I can give one of these brokers a name and address and, for a fee, he tells me how much money the person has in the bank," Beltrante said.

As a result of the Privacy Act and other federal regulations, Beltrante said that his agency used pretext interviews much more than previously. Whenever possible, he and his employees try to hold the interviews over the phone. He said he sees no problems with the ethics of posing as an old school friend or military companion to obtain information on the whereabouts, assets, marital status, or employment of people he needs to track down. The volume of work in private investigations has been increasing 10 to 15 percent each year, forcing companies like Beltrante's to use more pretext calls to obtain information for clients.

Openly or surreptitiously, investigators learn just about everything about you, and deliver that information to their clients—your new employer, the insurance company against whom you have a claim, or your banker who is considering granting you a major line of credit. How do they go about their work? Are the things they do legal? Can you prevent them from prying too deeply?

Today's 50,000 private investigators are increasingly adopting high-tech methods, including the use of computers, surveillance devices, and polygraph machines.

Flourishing investigative firms offer widely diverse clients a broad range of services concerning the personal backgrounds of individuals. These include pre-employment investigations, undercover work to spot employee dishonesty, background reports on credit and insurance applicants, investigations of insurance and worker's compensation claims, and screening of potential tenants for landlords. About 50 percent of an investigative firm's work involves background investigations of individuals and business firms.

According to the Office of Personnel Management, the federal government contracts with individual private investigators to help determine the suitability of federal job applicants. During fiscal year 1986, the 500 full-time investigators of the personnel office supplemented by 400 full- and part-time investigators hired under contract conducted background checks that included field investigations on 35,000 individuals. In 1986, the government commissioned private firms, such as Pinkerton's, Inc., the Wackenhut Corporation, Wells Fargo Guard Services, and Intertech, to ease the backlog of cases. Unlike consumer reporting personnel, agents employed by investigative reporting firms are apt to be well trained in methods of information collecting, although critics charge many are inadequately briefed and monitored on what constitutes lawful data collection procedures. A high percentage of private investigators have prior experience with state and local law enforcement departments or the FBI and use the training in their work.

A U.S. Department of Justice survey found that four out of ten private investigation firms employed off-duty police officers. In a 1985 report of the survey findings, the Justice Department warned that police information could easily be obtained in order for these individuals to "gain favor with their secondary employer." According to the report, "the potential for misuse of police information by 'moonlighting' officers in their contacts with private security provides sufficient justification for an effective department policy in this area."

According to a thirty-five-year veteran investigator, a highly devoted "buddy system" has evolved between active law enforcement officials and those who have retired or resigned from the service. Occasionally, these investigators even break the law to help one another. To obtain financial records, the private investigator turns to the security officers of banks, many of whom used to be on the same police force with him. Police officers and private investigators have been known to overlook criminal acts in exchange for cooperation and information, he asserts.

The Myth of Personal Privacy

According to Irwin Blye, head of a New York City-based investigative firm, "privacy is an absolute myth. When you're born, the first thing they do is take a footprint and fill out a birth certificate. You go to a doctor, they keep medical records. You go to school, they keep school records. You go to work, you buy a car or a house, there are more records. Your life is continuously open." Blye discussed information-gathering methods with my research assistant in August 1987.

Challenged to prove his contention that, given a little time and his usual fee, he could learn all about an individual without even speaking with him, Blye was presented with a subject—a New Jersey newspaperman—and his regular several-hundred-dollar-fee to perform a standard background investigation. The result was a five-page, single-spaced, typed report which documented, though not always accurately, a wide sweep of the journalist's past, and was detailed to the point of disclosing his father's income before his retirement.

Blye said that because of the methods his company uses to obtain information, laws such as the Privacy Act and others have not made his job more difficult. "The situation is the same as before. There is a wealth of information. But, the question is how to find the best way to get the answers." Blye said he tries to use only legal sources, and that he usually can get everything he needs without turning to subterfuge. He also said much confidential information can be obtained in public records. "If you go to see the records of a small-town water company, you can often see an unlisted phone number, former addresses, income, bank accounts, and many other very personal details about an individual. They are right there, but most people would never think of looking." Blye knows that many other private investigators use illegal or unauthorized sources to obtain information, but says that he has built up a reputation for operating "clean." "It's just a matter of time and effort, but it can be done. We try to do everything within what we have to work with," Blye explained.

Recently, Blye said, he has been able to obtain bank records simply by calling a bank employee and requesting the information. According to Blye, by dialing a number slightly different than the bank's main switchboard number and "sounding knowledgeable," he can easily persuade bank employees to give out customers' personal data. When trying to locate a savings account in addition to a regular checking account for example, Blye asks, "Can you tell me of any accommodations made on account with so and so?" The employee then is happy to cooperate. "They read it right off the computer screen to me!" Blye says there is nothing illegal with this practice that "makes the banks furious."

In other matters, Blye might use pretext interviews. "You do use them on certain things," he said, "but it depends on the case. For instance, I'm doing a background investigation on someone's daughter, and she is going with a young man and I want to know about his family. I may go into the neighborhood and canvass the area as if I am an insurance investigator looking for a witness to an accident. You'd be surprised the amount of information I'll get."

Record Searches

The individual rarely realizes the number of records held by city, county, state, and federal agencies that are open to investigators and anybody else for public inspection. These may include police arrest blotters, civil and criminal court records, motor vehicle accident reports, records of driving convictions, and possibly even welfare rolls or other records involving contacts with social service agencies. This information is available legally in most cases. Where it is not legally accessible, other means may be used by some investigators.

Adverse information is regarded as especially useful. A report containing negative information covering morals, business reputation, and domestic problems can be prepared solely on the basis of public records. Mindful of this, some investigative agencies place increased emphasis on public-record reporting. "This is the future of the investigative business," notes one company's chief executive. He encourages investigators to "use these reports and stop making everybody liable for all kinds of problems."

Public Good vs. Private Need

Security industry spokespersons, along with the nation's retailers, distributors, and manufacturers, make a good case for the private sector's need for investigative services. This need was supported by a study conducted by the Rand Corporation that stated, "private security services fill a perceived need and provide clear social benefits to their consumers and, to some extent, to the general public. Few would argue that if private security services were drastically reduced or eliminated, reported crime, fear of crime, and prices of merchandise would rise." According to a 1985 U.S. Department of Justice report, the private security business is one of the nation's top ten fastest-growing service industries. Those employed as private investigators or security guards now outnumber all publicly paid police by at least two to one. In some states, the ratio is as high as five to one. In 1986, public police forces in the United States were paid about $15 billion while about $25 billion was spent on private security protection.

In a dramatic case, a judge awarded over $13 million to a man whose wife was raped and murdered by an employee of a furniture-leasing company who had a prior felony conviction. An executive of a major private security and investigative organization stated during his testimony before the USPPC that this was believed to be "the first case in Maryland centering on the issue of whether an employer has the duty to investigate prospective employees who would deal with the public. The suit accused the furniture company of negligence in its hiring and supervision practices because it failed to investigate the employee. Unknown to the company, the employee had been convicted of armed robbery in the District of Columbia and was on parole when he committed the murder."

Obviously, it is important to establish rules so that the business community—and hence indirectly the public—receives every reasonable and practical protection against the dishonest and criminal element in our society. On the other hand, it is essential that the individual be extended maximum reasonable safeguards against possible security industry abuses due to overzealousness, human error, or ignorance.

"Nature and Certainty"

"Nature and certainty," said the Roman emperor and philosopher Marcus Antonius, "are very hard to come at."

With streams of information being fed into America's data banks annually, some of it is bound to be false or misleading. Where medical information is involved, for example, all of it should come from professionally reliable sources. The collection of technical data from anyone other than the individual himself, a medical source, or a close family member invites inaccuracies. Some reporting companies requiring information, however, may interview the applicant's neighbors, friends, and associates, and thereby get a layman's personal interpretation of medical evidence instead of the facts. Once a misstatement gets into the file, it is copied and distributed again and again so that its adverse effect tends to proliferate.

How Some Investigators Work

In the past, the Federal Trade Commission had found that some employees of one of the largest investigating companies in the nation had misrepresented themselves as insurance company employees, encouraged other employees to produce adverse reports about consumers, implied to customers that certain consumers' files contained adverse information that could not be released because it extended beyond the Fair Credit Reporting Act's seven-year deadline, and committed other violations.

In sworn testimony before the USPPC, a former western regional manager of an investigative firm which had annual revenues of about $3 million was asked to describe how medical information was acquired without authorization. He said it was done primarily by telephone, in which the investigator would record both sides of the conversation. For example, he would call the hospital's medical records department posing as a doctor. In most cases, he could convince the medical records librarian, secretary, or clerk that he was a medical man and was able to get the desired information. The approach was usually successful, he said, because the investigators were well trained by the company. The training generally took about a year.

The testimony about the training included this exchange:
QUESTION: There are training manuals put out by the company?
ANSWER: Right.
Q: The training manuals explain how to call and pretend to be a doctor?
A: Right.
Q: Did they instruct investigators to keep their techniques and activities under their hat?
A: Oh, yes.

If the sham failed, the investigator would wait two or three days and then go to a hospital "source." The source, who could be a hospital employee or doctor's secretary, often would disclose the information requested by telephone, mail, or in response to the investigator's personal visit.

Q: Did you authorize payment to her [the source]?
A: Yes.
Q: What was the total amount [that the company] paid for its investigation and acquisition of medical records, approximately?
A: There were three different billings, total of approximately $1,500.
Q: Of that, how much did [the source] get?
A: As I recall, it was around between $150 and $200.

The witness further testified that they would go so far as to create and use phony subpoenas. He explained that information from the Internal Revenue Service, Social Security Administration, and motor vehicle bureaus could be obtained by his posing as an IRS agent or employee of one of the services. You simply "rattle off the driver's license or social security number—they don't question it," he said. "You use the most convenient identity and receive highly personal information about income and finances just by asking for it."

Q: Were there any hospitals in the area that you could not get records from in one of the ways described?
A: Over a period of time and after constant pounding of one shape, form, or fashion, 99 percent of the time it could be achieved one way or the other. There have been times calls were made at one and two o'clock in the morning after the shift changes when the librarian and the file clerks are not so alert. . . .

He testified further: "Whatever information they needed and whatever pretext they needed, they used it, because they had been instructed—see, this instruction is not only on medical, it's everything. It's how to be a police officer, how to be a welfare officer, how to be anything, any social officer, internal revenue. Whatever you needed, you were instructed before."

One eight-page report of medical information obtained by such techniques contained a detailed description of a psychiatric patient's history, condition, and diagnosis. It disclosed that the desertion of the woman by her husband brought on a "psychotic depressive reaction" and that she was admitted to the hospital for "acute symptoms of gastroenteritis." It provided comments about the subject and her husband, and even revealed that the patient was billed $3,991.36 for psychiatric services. In reporting this information to its client, the investigative company boasted: "We might add that under the California statutes, psychiatrists will not give out information on a patient's treatment, even with authorization. If they do so, they can be subjected to a $500 fine."

In another case, the investigator reported to his client: "Somewhat perturbed at this lack of cooperation on both the part of the doctor and this hospital, we decided to quit wasting time to obtain records legitimately, and once again directed our sources to pull the chart on the sly and photograph all of the relevant parts." The report further states: "In the matter of obtaining records, we are customarily requested by clients to determine medical information without authorization and have managed to develop very good channels over the years for this type of procurement."

It is especially sobering that professional investigators succeed in getting medical information from doctors' offices and health-care institutions over 90 percent of the time. As a rule, the larger the institution, the easier it is to get the information. Apparently these techniques are possible because of the laxness of health-care providers and other associated institutions.

Investigative companies recognize the impropriety of selling some types of information. A confidential medical report and chart obtained by one investigator was stamped with the warning, "We should caution the readers that this document is intended for your use only and should not be divulged in detail to other parties. The chart in question [hospital chart attached to the report] is extremely personal and of a volatile nature, and should be treated as privileged information."

Investigative companies are hardly shy about advertising their special capabilities to potential clients. One instructed its investigators thus: "I would strongly suggest writing a letter to the manager advising him that we do many assignments for [name of company] relative to obtaining medical information without authorization." And the company's sales brochure stated: "Also, we at times pay source fees for confidential police information, MVD sources, et cetera. Our company has specialized in obtaining school and employment records."

When the informant was asked if he ever discussed this practice with his supervisors, he answered, "Never in detail. We were always—that was kind of kept away from us. It was never brought up. It was kind of like the less you know, the better off you are, and they did the instructing, and if you didn't do it according to their rules and methods, you ended up like I did— [fired]."

Investigative firms will sometimes do anything they have to when on deadline for a client. "It is of the utmost urgency," wrote a company manager, "[that] you furnish us your report promptly. Please note that you have been looking into medical aspects of this case for three months, which certainly should be sufficient to acquire the medical record and forward it to us. In addition, we want to know what the current activities are. . . ."

He received back a report labeled "PRIVILEGED-CONFIDENTIAL." Although unauthorized by the claimant to receive information, the investigative firm wrote: "Utilizing medical sources, inquiry was made at this hospital facility concerning the care and treatment of your subject and we are advised of the following. . . ." The "following" included a detailed description of the patient's hospital admission, medical symptoms, treatment, diagnosis, and employment status. The woman herself did not have this information, but her insurance company did, and so did its attorney.

In one imaginative example of a pretext interview, the subject of an investigation received a telephone call at his home from a person who identified himself as a court official wanting to know why a jury duty questionnaire was not answered. When the subject denied having received the questionnaire, the caller said, "Well, all right, we can complete it over the telephone." The investigator then proceeded to ask all kinds of personal questions and subsequently entered the subject's answers in his investigative report.

Surreptitious Techniques

Clearly, it is much easier in some situations to get information when an investigator is disguised as a police officer, telephone repairman, doctor, nurse, clergyman, or janitor than to admit that he or she is an investigator. For example, an undercover agent appeared in the office of a large corporation just prior to closing time with an attache case under his arm. Heading for the men's room, he waited in a booth until everyone left. Then, removing a pair of coveralls from the attache case, he put them on, and stashed his jacket in the case. After slipping the coveralls on, he hid the attache case behind a trash container and left the men's room. Now, posing as a member of the after-hours cleaning crew, and equipped with a miniature but powerful camera, he entered the individual offices at will and searched the files without challenge.

Along with the security industry in general, support organizations are available. One example is the "spy school." Some schools feature the very latest in undercover investigation, industrial espionage technology, and electronic surveillance. In these schools, students learn about magnetic tape, transmitters, and receivers. They study the use of body bugs and the applications of night-vision devices. Schools also detail how phones are bugged, how rooms are bugged, and then how to debug the room and "sweep" the telephone line using electronic countermeasures.

Surveillance technology has made giant strides, employing and surpassing many of the techniques developed during World War II, the Korean War, and the Vietnam War. The non-military use of much of this technology has been encouraged by the law enforcement and criminal justice community, and to some extent is passed along to the private sector. About 100,000 electronic eavesdropping devices have been illegally planted in U.S. businesses within the last several years. Corporate conference rooms, boardrooms, and computer centers are being bugged every day.

Most notable perhaps among the diverse and flexible characteristics of electronic surveillance are the advances in miniaturization which allow equipment to be easily concealed, producing, for example, a microphone that fits into the cavity of a tooth. Modular systems can be expanded and augmented quickly and simply, with devices and equipment activated automatically. A sensing device added to a tape recorder, for example, can be automatically triggered by a human voice.

"Bugs" made almost any size are relatively easy to build and widely available. Transmitters tied to a power source, such as an electrical wire or telephone line, can transmit indefinitely. Telephone microphones can transmit voices even when the receiver is on the hook. Methods of hiding these devices are getting more sophisticated as well. Microphone wires, which are smaller than a human hair, are virtually impossible to detect when painted over after they are in place. Epoxy encapsulation makes bugs indistinguishable from surrounding surfaces. When hidden behind the wall with only a tiny hole the size of a pencil point drilled through, bugs can be almost invisible.

Bugs also come in a variety of designs. One high-tech device bounces a laser beam off a window pane and allows conversations in a closed room to be monitored. Harry Augenblick, president of Microlab/FXR, a Livingston, New Jersey, security firm, described one bug he called a "picture-hook bug." According to Augenblick, the bug is slipped into the wall just as a regular picture hanger would be. After the picture is hung back on the wall, the bug might go unnoticed for years.

Your Sometimes-Not-So-Friendly Neighbor

A wag once defined a neighbor as a person who can get to your house in less than a minute and take two hours to get back home. It is sometimes surprising how much he is likely to learn during those visits about your living habits, personal problems, day-to-day behavior, and activities.

According to at least one investigator, people love to talk about their neighbors if drawn out shrewdly. He added, "My job would be a lot tougher without this all-too-common human failing." Neighbors' hidden feelings of jealousy or resentment may be expressed through shrewd questioning. Equally injurious to the individual is the well-intentioned neighbor who innocently discloses information that may be incomplete, misleading, or false. Typical of most investigators, he said neighbors "can be extremely helpful, volunteering information about the times the subject leaves and returns home, the kind of friends he associates with, how well he gets along with his spouse, his financial condition, and general personal habits."

In one situation, a teenager visited the family doctor at the same time other youths his age were on hand awaiting treatment for drug addiction. A few minutes later, one of the teenager's neighbors who had an appointment with the doctor entered the waiting room. The teenager thought nothing of it at the time. Years later, however, when he was married, employed, and living comfortably, the incident surfaced. When he and his wife, expecting their first child, applied for life insurance, their application was rejected.

Stunned, he inquired and was told that in his record was adverse information stemming back to his old hometown and neighborhood. Tracking down the source, he learned that the informant was the neighbor who had seen him in the doctor's office with the known drug users. On the basis of an incorrect assumption, the neighbor had told the insurance investigator that he was "on drugs."

A field manual published by one of the larger investigative reporting organizations instructing employees on the techniques of eliciting information during interviews counsels that interviewers "must not be afraid to ask personal questions and should be sufficiently suspicious by nature to derive satisfaction from tracking down leads and developing the facts." It continues, "the top-notch field representative should be highly sensitive to the more subtle clues in the remarks of his sources and other behavior, perceiving their implications and adapting his own approach and conversation accordingly. . . . A sense of [being] human [will prove to be] a powerful instrument in the development of a warm, friendly relationship with sources. In fact some of the most pertinent personal information is sandwiched between homey remarks and other small talk."

Agents were encouraged to proceed from the impersonal to the personal approach. The manual cautions that people are reluctant to talk to strangers about the personal reputations and morals of their friends and acquaintances, and that starting with impersonal matters would put them off guard and so lower their hesitancy to become more personal after "the ice has been broken."

Open-ended questions were also recommended: "How is he regarded?" instead of "Is he well regarded?" "How much does he drink?" instead of

"Does he drink?" In many cases, the name of the client is not given to the source, and in some cases the source is not aware, even in a general sense, of the interview's purpose.

While conceding the need for investigative reporting services in our society, authorities are quick to point out that private agents have a vast potential to harm the reputation and pocketbook of the person under investigation. Some of the problems include inexperienced and inadequately trained personnel, agency employees who either disregard or are unfamiliar with lawful investigative procedures, and the relative absence of state regulation. These result in investigators inaccurately or falsely reporting, trespassing on private property to spy on or photograph the person being investigated, searching premises illegally when the person being investigated is absent, and posing as someone other than a private investigator when obtaining information from neighbors. Obviously, this is an area requiring constant vigilance by administrative, legislative, and judicial authorities, as well as personal alertness on the part of individual citizens. Here, a precise balance between personal privacy rights and unconventional, prying investigations must always be sought, but cannot always be fully achieved. Perhaps this is as it should be in our remarkable free society.

Conclusion

The steadily expanding private investigative industry employs some methods that break and circumvent existing laws. The modern investigator often is a highly trained professional with an arsenal of high-tech equipment at his disposal, working for private interests. Regardless of the methods used, the results are the same—the invasion of personal privacy.

Among the techniques used are pretext interviews of the unsuspecting subject and his acquaintances, and informal personal contacts with police, bankers, medical personnel, and government employees. "Spying" is occasionally used to obtain sensitive information which is not necessarily always accurate. No records are inviolate. "Confidential" financial records (even Swiss numbered bank accounts), medical information, and government records all have been obtained for a fee, without authorization.

Individuals should constantly be alert to possible abuses of their personal information, as well as information about others. Laws that already exist should be enforced vigorously. Employees in sensitive positions should be informed of existing laws. They should be alert to and informed about methods outsiders use to obtain unauthorized information.

12

Big Brother and How to Protect against Him

The greatest dangers to liberty lurk in insidious encroachment by men of zeal, well-meaning but without understanding.

—Louis D. Brandeis

The proper function of a government is to make it easy for the people to do good, and difficult for them to do evil.

—William Gladstone

Today, records determine relationships between you and the many organizations that are all around you. Their effect is quicker, broader, and more unfair than at any time in history.

"Big Brother is watching you" is the sinister theme overhanging George Orwell's oppressive society in his book *1984*, one of the best selling novels of our age. In it the author expresses his concern for what happens when the individual is influenced by the demands and interests of a large government or private organization. The book presents a vivid impression of the power of records and technology when used for surveillance and control purposes. The dominance by Big Brother is sustained and enhanced by his ability to collect information about individuals.

Some would argue that the book is not relevant in the United States today because of the protections guaranteed by the First Amendment (guaranteeing freedom of speech, assembly, etc.), Fourth Amendment (prohibiting unreasonable searches and seizures), Fifth Amendment (against self-incrimination), and mechanisms such as the Freedom of Information Act and the Privacy Act of 1974. These are obvious elements that operate against personal and privacy abuse. Clearly, political and legal guarantees are engrained in the fabric of the American political culture.

It does not follow, however, that the absence of visible oppression assures liberty, privacy, individualism, and human dignity. When we delve into the constitutional, legislative, and judicial protections, some of the more subtle forms of potential and real abuse begin to surface.

Were Orwell alive today, I believe he would be motivated to put forward the same message. Because we enjoy procedural guarantees of freedom, we often become insensitive to the forces that covertly mold our attitudes and influence personal actions. It was James Madison in 1788 when addressing the Virginia Convention who warned, "There are more instances of the abridgement of the freedom of the people by gradual and silent encroachments of those in power than by violent and sudden usurpations." Every day we learn of what some argue are constitutional violations by officials by silent encroachments. We learn how frequently those in high public and private office abuse their trusts, reaching even into the White House.

Computers and Politics

The computer is being used as a tool for influencing voters. For example, Matt Reese, William Hamilton, and Jonathan Robbin developed a computer system called Geodemographics that classifies people for direct-mail campaigns. The system is partially based on the fact that the economic and social characteristics of most American neighborhoods are very similar. The developers analyze information about income, education, and the make-up of the people who live in the approximately 43,000 census tracts in the United States, and operate on the basis that people often group themselves in areas where their resources match their needs. The system was successfully used to persuade voters to reject right-to-work legislation in Missouri, and is being used by many in congressional reelection bids.

Information regarding the likes and dislikes, the political leanings, and preferences of Americans is so comprehensive that in some cases an election is determined before the voting begins. The concern for the impact of the computer on our form of government had reached the point several years ago that the Senate Governmental Affairs Committee had directed a study to determine whether computers are upsetting the balance of power between the legislative and executive branches of government.

The world's information base is now estimated to be doubling every three to four years. Information is power, and the ever-increasing capability of organizations to collect, store, and transmit information has serious implications for our separation of powers. The executive branch has a clear advantage in this regard. A recent study by the Office of Technology Assessment estimated that by the year 1990, there will be over half a million central processing units in the executive branch of the federal government. This explosion of computers magnifies the opportunities for misuse manyfold.

Congress itself has also become more computerized. The principle use to date is to generate mailing lists for the individual legislator to target supporters. Political scientists argue that direct mailings to constituents increase the advantages of incumbency and have contributed to the decline of marginal congressional districts.

Congress has also taken steps to bring computers into the policy-making process. Since 1985, both Washington and state offices have been equipped with powerful data-management systems to analyze the volume of background material available on issues, constituents, and colleagues.

Now that congressmen have this full computer capability, how will sensitive information be used? Will the congressman most adept at using the computerized sensitive personal information about the voting public and his congressional peers enable him to dominate that representative body?

Observing these phenomena and relating them to Orwell's work, Walter Cronkite in the preface to the 1983 edition of Orwell's *1984* noted that the book is in effect a warning that modern man "may be neither strong enough, nor wise enough, nor moral enough to cope" with this kind of increase in technological power. The lesson is not that technology is inherently evil, but that it may make possible the alteration of social relations in ways that we may not understand or even realize. Perceptive journalist David Burnham warns, "The loss of privacy is a key symptom of one of the fundamental social problems of our age: the growing power of large public and private institutions in relation to the individual citizen."

Electronic Surveillance

We are, thankfully, a long way from the situation in which "Big Brother is watching you" for ulterior purposes. On the other hand, there was no technology used by Big Brother or his followers that is not now in place or at least feasible. The Orwellian society, if not politically, is at least technologically possible.

Modern technology makes it more efficient and less conspicuous to track movements, to hear conversations, to know the details of financial and other personal transactions, and to combine information from diverse sources into a composite file. While the precise extent of use of electronic surveillance by the private sector is unknown, a 1985 study by the Office of Technology Assessment determined that about 25 percent of federal agency components engage in some current or planned use of various electronic surveillance technologies. These uses are concentrated in components of the departments of Justice, Treasury, Defense, Agriculture, and Interior.

The Advisory Policy Board of the National Crime Information Center recently gave preliminary approval to a proposal to expand the present computer file. The Information Center, which is managed by the Federal Bureau of Investigation, would then have the capability to track the movements of people under suspicion of a crime but who had not been charged. The proposed expansion also covers "people on probation or parole, people who 'are a danger to law-enforcement officers' and people who are known or suspected 'operatives of foreign governments.' " The advisory panel also suggested that the file should have electronic access to records of other government agencies, such as the IRS, Immigration and Naturalization Service, and the passport office.

Mini-satellites read the license plates of an automobile or spot a person from miles in the sky. Today they are being used for surveillance of drug traffickers and for other law enforcement purposes. Will they always be so used?

Telemetric tracking devices attached to subjects transmit the location and physiological condition of the wearers. These devices are being used officially in at least eleven locations in Colorado, Florida, Illinois, Oregon, Pennsylvania, and British Columbia. In most cases, court-supervised sentences stipulate that the lawbreaker wear an anklet containing an electronic transmitter. The signal is picked up on a computer, and the judge receives a daily printout. The devices are "transforming the future of corrections," says Dick Jorandby, public defender in Florida's Palm Beach County, site of the first "electronic house arrest" pilot test. In Palm Beach County alone, about 190 offenders have worn the special ankle bracelets since 1984.

Transmitting devices the size of a thermostat are now hidden in some automobiles and give off a signal that can be activated by a state police computer. Each transmitter has a unique five-digit code which is compared with the vehicle identification number in the police crime computer. Police cars equipped with tracking computers home in on the transmitted signals. The police thereby are able to track precisely where the vehicle is at all times. These devices are now operating throughout Massachusetts and parts of Florida. They are also slated for use in New Jersey and California. At one time Massachusetts Governor Michael S. Dukakis indicated he would like to have such a device installed in all cars manufactured in this country. Will we have adequate enforcible controls to assure that these devices will not be abused? We don't have those controls yet, nor are any being planned.

The use of electronic paging devices has grown significantly and is expected to increase in the near future. The development of more sophisticated pagers with the ability to receive messages is currently underway. The technology already exists to intercept messages transmitted to such devices.

The number of federal court-approved bugs and videotapes in 1984 was the highest ever. Furthermore, provisions in the Electronic Communications Privacy Act of 1986 make it easier for law enforcement officials to get approval to tap phones in the future.

Although use of some surveillance techniques requires a court order, many do not require any authorized approval and some are not even covered by judicial interpretation of the Fourth Amendment prohibition of unreasonable searches and seizures. Additionally, the privacy and procedural rights of those subject to surveillance may also be violated, since their activities may be monitored even though they are not under any criminal suspicion. Finally, given the unobtrusive nature of surveillance activities, it is often difficult to detect when your rights are being violated.

Direct, physical surveillance devices have been proliferating. The city of Charleston, West Virginia, is currently using video cameras in its downtown surveillance program to deter crime and furnish the police with evidence on offenders. The system uses zoom lenses which enable police to identify suspects at distances up to three blocks from the cameras. Although some residents have objected to the use of television surveillance, police officials say that since their introduction in mid-1985, the cameras have led to several arrests and have furnished evidence on drug traffic, assaults, and other crimes. One-way video has entered most banks and shopping malls. Personal truth technology, such as polygraphs and voice-stress analyzers, is widely used. There already have been developed computerized devices that can read your lips. Other machines can accurately imitate your voice.

Two-way cable television allows viewers immediately to answer questions or order products. With such systems, a computer is able to record what people buy, how much they spend, what they watch, how they paid their bills, and where the money came from. It also knows when they come home and how many people are in the house. As a result, some see possible dangers in two-way wired television systems, and Congress enacted the Cable Franchise Policy and Communication Act of 1984 in an attempt to forestall abuses. The act places restrictions on collection, use, and disclosure of data about subscribers.

Most forms of electronic communications—whether via wire, coaxial cable, microwave, satellite, or even fiber optics—can be monitored.

The Electronic Communications Privacy Act of 1986 made some substantial improvements in protecting communication transmitted over media such as fiber-optic, microwave, and digital electronic systems. Other aspects of the legislation however have caused critics to call the law "a Trojan horse." The legislation specifically exempted the wireless portion of cellular telephone transmissions, as well as tone-only paging devices. Furthermore, the law made it easier for law enforcement offices to obtain permission to eavesdrop on individual and corporate communications. Finally, the law allows the FBI to hire independent contractors to carry out this monitoring in order to "free field agents from the relatively routine activity of monitoring interception."

It might be noted—with some concern—that the Federal Bureau of Investigation engages in so much private communications monitoring that the task is considered a "relatively routine activity" and that it finds it necessary to contract out some of this surveillance. This creates an additional potential for privacy abuse from improper management of data when it is in the hands of private contractors.

Government officials may install pen registers after first obtaining a court order. Pen registers are devices attached to a telephone line to record numbers that are dialed and the length of the phone call. With a reverse phone book, one can then determine the party that was called.

Investigative authorities can generally get access to information that the telephone company retains for billing purposes with a court order under a grand jury subpoena, which does not require probable cause.

Among other things, Orwell and others have been trying to warn that man may be trapped into succumbing to the clutches of Big Brother through computers that listen in on any or all personal telephone conversations and watch our movements by satellites from miles in the sky. We know that interactive television transmits and records what programs we watch, and where we are in our homes. Credit cards trace our economic paths for they are, in effect, personal financial diaries.

One writer believes that in the future, large-scale automated transaction systems called cryptosystems may be designed which would protect and maintain the security of individuals and organizations in their dealings with each other. This approach is supposed to allow individuals and the organizations they deal with to exchange only information that is relevant to the particular transaction. The use of pseudonyms, he maintains, prevents unauthorized inquiry into an individual's personal privacy. The developer of the system thinks the use of unlinkable pseudonyms would provide credentialing and payment transfers with "unconditional untraceability." When interfacing with record-keeping systems, individuals would use different account numbers or digital pseudonyms with each organization. While pseudonyms may be used just one time, for a series of transactions such as with a bank account, a single pseudonym could be used repeatedly. Credit or identification cards would be replaced by a personal card computer resembling a credit-card-sized calculator. The card computer would be used to make transactions just as automatic tellers and point-of-sale terminals are today. Whether such a system can be made workable is open to question.

In the past, information existing in manually recorded form did not threaten the individual's private life to a significant extent. Now, organizational memories are extended over time and space. Whole personal profiles may be constructed by linking credit, banking, medical, educational, employment, tax, criminal, or welfare records.

The implications of the existence and availability of this kind of personal information was vividly expressed by Alexander Solzhenitsyn: "As every man goes through life he fills in a number of forms for the record, each containing a number of questions. . . . There are thus hundreds of little threads radiating from every man, millions of threads in all. . . . They are not visible, they are not material. . . . Each man, permanently aware of his own invisible threads, naturally develops a respect for the people who manipulate the threads." Manipulation of information, Orwell wrote, can be as deadly as the bearing of arms. His work is a renewed call for eternal vigilance to protect our freedoms against the relentless encroachment of the large organization.

It is a call for the maintenance of an equitable balance between individual rights and the needs of powerful organizations. Such a balance can be reached only by many painstaking judgments and evaluations of specific issues at hand. Personal privacy is a basic force and need in democratic life. One treads on the most sensitive ground in attempting to weigh the issue of individual freedom and privacy against the societal need for services effectively rendered. Tradeoffs are unavoidable, tradeoffs that must be objectively measured in the executive, legislative, and judicial chambers of the land. "Government is a contrivance of human wisdom to provide for human wants," wrote Edmund Burke. "Men have a right that these wants should be provided for by this wisdom." Clearly, collectively we must strive to adequately provide for our privacy needs by accommodating the conflicting interests of society. Its achievement could be an endless process.

Standards for Organizational Behavior

Organization administrators, including employers, should not await a government mandate but should address this concern. Every effort should be made to protect the privacy of individuals while meeting the legitimate needs of business, government, and society for information. Every institution can reap considerable goodwill and operational benefits by adopting fair information practices to help ensure the protection of the privacy rights of all individuals with whom it comes in contact.

Fair information practices fall into three general categories: gathering only accurate and pertinent information; granting individuals access to records of which they are the subject; and limiting access to data by third parties. Specific guidelines for organizational behavior follow:

1. *Acquire only relevant information.* Doing so reduces the amount of personal information in circulation, thereby reducing the potential for abuse, and assures that decisions will be based solely on pertinent data. Appropriate steps must be taken to ensure the accuracy of acquired information.

Citicorp policy demonstrates a workable system in which no more information than is needed is acquired. Their consumer pamphlet *Strictly Confidential—How Citibank Protects Your Privacy*, issued several years ago, states:

> What we ask you depends on what you ask of us. If you're buying travelers checks, for example, all we need is your signature to identify you, and your address, to contact you if we recover checks you lose.
>
> To open a savings account, we ask for enough information to be sure we give your money to the right person, your address to mail your statements, and your social security number to report the interest we pay you to the Internal Revenue Service.
>
> A checking account involves the risk of overdrawn accounts, so we also require references, such as your employer or a bank where you had an account before.
>
> If you ask for credit, we need more information. Some we need to comply with laws. For example, the law governs how much we can lend for certain purposes and requires us to report lending for some purposes; so we must ask the purpose of the loan. But mainly, we want enough information to be reasonably sure you will repay the obligation.

2. *Consider pretext interviews unacceptable methods of gathering information.* The use of pretext interviews is illegal conduct in some jurisdictions and unethical behavior in all. Furthermore, such practices invite inaccurate and misleading information when the informant believes that he is providing information within a context which is quite different from that in which it will ultimately be used.

3. *Use no polygraph or other lie detector tests in employment.* Chapter 3 outlined the inaccuracy, impersonality, and intimidation inherent in such tests. Dishonesty and employee theft can be reduced through careful screening and interviewing of applicants, improving employer-employee relations, and personal observation and investigation. Such efforts may be rewarded with a happier, more productive work force. Courts almost uniformly refuse to admit test results as evidence of guilt or innocence.

4. *Allow and encourage employees and consumers to see and copy records pertaining to them.* Certain information such as employee evaluations and investigatory proceedings may be excepted from this requirement, but such exceptions should be as narrowly tailored as possible.

5. *Keep no secret records.* The nature of all information systems should be disclosed. If it is imperative that particular data be classified or access be otherwise restricted, under no circumstances should the *existence* of records be hidden.

6. *Establish a procedure for challenging and correcting erroneous reports.* Be reluctant to substitute records for face-to-face contact. First-hand information provided by the subject of a report should be given full consideration, unless discredited by significant legitimate evidence. In this manner, not only will the privacy rights of the individual be respected, but the organization can be sure that it is acting upon accurate information.

7. *Use information only for the purpose for which it was originally acquired.* Information can assume unexpected and at times damaging aspects when viewed in contexts other than that in which it was originally solicited. Allow limited access to data by staff members. Maintain only information necessary for day-to-day transactions in current files.

8. *Transfer no information without the subjects' authorization or knowledge.* Much information is provided freely because of an implicit expectation of confidentiality. Once again, Citicorp espouses the norm which other businesses and agencies could emulate:

> Citicorp will respond in general terms to traditional credit inquiries, but our policy is and will continue to be to hold in confidence specific information about our business relationship with a customer—individual, commercial, or governmental—and not to disclose such information to anyone else except to the extent that the customer agrees or the law requires. We do not honor requests for information about a customer merely because the person asking for it may ultimately be able to obtain a subpoena or because we are trying to be "cooperative." No law requires us to give anyone your personal records without their going through a legal process and giving us a legal order. . . . We give the government only what the law requires us to—no more, no less. If a legal process requires us to disclose the affairs of a customer to anyone, unless a government agency certifies to us in writing that it has already notified the customer, it is our general policy to send the customer notice of the fact.

9. *Destroy data after its purpose has been served.* Regularly purge records and destroy those that are of no further use and that are no longer required by law. Program computers to destroy outdated records. This will ensure that data will not be used without authorization, or for purposes other than for the purpose collected.

The Tradeoffs

Is the question, "What price privacy?" a fair question to ask? Must the question be answered with a cost-benefit analysis before mandating individual privacy protections? No more so than if we answer, "What price liberty?" only after a cost-benefit analysis and only then agree to establish constitutional, legislative, and administrative protections. Or, for that matter, if we ask, "What price freedom of speech, assembly, or religion?" In a totalitarian society, the first right to go is the right of privacy. Can we risk losing that right to the principal of cost-benefit?

A fifty-year-old Leningrad-born Soviet Jewish emigré, an engineer by profession, recorded his reflections on life in the Soviet Union for the William E. Wiener Oral History Library of the American Jewish Committee. "There is no such thing as privacy in the Soviet Union. There is no Russian word for it as you have in English, and the right to it is not given in the constitution. The right to privacy would be contradictory to the spirit of Soviet life. Everything in America is done for the individual. Individuality is a big thing. In the Soviet Union the individual is nothing. The community is everything."

Another societal tradeoff weighs an individual's privacy rights against the citizen's right of protection from crime. Law enforcement officials make it clear that any curb on their efforts to identify and apprehend criminals favors the law breaker and is detrimental to crime's innocent victims. State laws dealing with sensitive law enforcement issues vary widely. Public policy for a social issue in our dynamic democracy only blossoms into full bloom in stages, over a long period of time. As occurred with the issue of civil rights, personal initiatives and administrative actions together with legislative mandates and judicial decisions eventually contributed to the final mosaic. So will it be with the issue of privacy.

One possible alternative to the endless erosion of personal privacy through increased surveillance suggested by some writers is for organizations to relax the differences which they seek to make in their treatment of people. Pursuit of such less information-intensive alternatives would entail fundamental change in peoples' expectations of organizations. By minimizing differences in how people are treated in light of their records, the necessity for developing such records would be minimized. The question is, of course, can our complex society function effectively if substantial quantities of personal data were not available? I think not, in view of the high expectations from society, government, and business, and the resulting myriad decisions that have to be made by those who approve bank and mortgage loans, insurance applications, school admissions, government loan guarantees, welfare applications, and innumerable other programs.

Over two decades ago, sociologist Edward McDonagh in studying how people manage to cope with the sometimes inhuman tumult and personal intrusiveness of our mass society found that mentally soothing snatches of privacy are being grasped by the individual in his automobile. He observed, "You find it driving to work, alongside all those other people, but alone with your thoughts. The car has become a secular sanctuary for the individual, his shrine to the self, his mobile Walden Pond." Such an approach is, as Emerson has written, more like having one enclosed "in a tumultuous privacy of storm." Obviously this kind of temporary withdrawal is not the answer. Sporadic withdrawal may give some physical respite for those with automobiles who spend time every day doing routine driving on sparsely traveled highways, but don't try it in Manhattan, Chicago, or Los Angeles!

To honor our heritage of individual freedom requires that we be willing to adopt discreet procedures, regulations, and/or laws so that there is the kind of orderly, sensitive accumulation and use of personal information that assures the protection of privacy rights. Life in a democracy requires both freedom and order. As educator Roger William Heyns has written, "Freedom presupposes order, and order presupposes rules and the ability to enforce them." Rules for privacy protection and the ability to enforce them in the United States are found wanting. Yet, it was Supreme Court Justice William O. Douglas who counseled, "Privacy is the penumbra of the Bill of Rights."

Government and corporate information privacy protection actions are in evolutionary stages. Meanwhile, there are personal initiatives that are available to the individual. A number of basic guidelines have been implemented in varying degrees by many. Each of us can take the initiative to seek to apply them on our own in our everyday dealings to help protect against the unrelenting seepage of these personal rights.

Basic Guidelines for Protection of Your Personal Privacy

1. Give out only that information about yourself, family, and friends that is relevant to the decision at hand.

2. In all interviews, try to satisfy yourself that the true purpose is as stated by the interviewer.

3. Challenge the need to sign waivers giving others access to personal information about you whenever you can. If you do sign a waiver, insist on a time limitation. Make sure the waiver is not a blanket permission to turn over information about you to any third party requesting it. Whenever possible, designate that it applies only to a specifically named organization or individual.

4. Find out what sources will be contacted to get information about you, how the data will be used, and to whom it will be disclosed.

5. Ask the receiver of the personal information to use it only for the purpose it is collected.

6. Ask to see and copy records about yourself from any organization that keeps a file on you. Seek to correct the record if you find it inaccurate.

7. Be alert to try to discover any files about you being kept in secret for any reason whatsoever. Assert your desire to know all about them.

8. Ask those to whom you give personal, sensitive information to get your approval before transferring it to anyone else.

9. Ask those to whom you give sensitive information to destroy it after its usefulness has ended.

10. Request that government officials who want access to your records held by a third party present proper authorization before being permitted to do so, and request to be notified when such disclosure is made by others.

11. The Fourth Amendment to the United States Constitution specifies that you are guaranteed freedom from "unreasonable searches and seizures." Thus, with a few exceptions, your home cannot be entered and searched without a search warrant signed by a judge unless you give your personal permission to do so. If evidence against you is obtained in an illegal search, it cannot be used against you in court. Don't inadvertently waive this protection by voluntarily opening your premises to intruders.

12. Be discreet and thoughtful about the information you disclose to others about yourself, friends, and neighbors. You are not necessarily being patriotic in mindlessly furnishing government personnel more information than they require. On the contrary, by so doing you may be creating the potential for undercutting the very foundation upon which our freedoms are built.

13. Remain vigilant. Remember, the first right to go in a totalitarian society is the right of individual privacy. Privacy is the vestibule of freedom.

To enjoy the many benefits of our individual-centered society requires the ongoing examination of the basic values that our heritage and Constitution represent, balancing them with the material benefits given us by free enterprise linked to never-ending scientific breakthroughs. Freedom is like a rope made of several strands. Weaken or remove one strand, and the rope is weakened.

There are bad people in the world, ever watchful for opportunities to seize dominance over others. For good people to stand idly by is to welcome the erosion and eventual collapse of all our freedoms.

Index

A Note on the Author

David F. Linowes is Professor of Political Economy and Public Policy, and Boeschenstein Professor Emeritus at the University of Illinois. He is also Senior Advisor to the Institute of Government and Public Affairs.

Prior to joining the university in 1976, he was national partner of a worldwide management consulting firm. Professor Linowes served as Chairman of the U.S. Privacy Protection Commission from 1975 to 1977. He chaired the President's Commission on the Nation's Energy Resources from 1981 to 1982, and the President's Commission on Privatization from 1987 to 1988. He headed economic development missions for the U.S. Department of State and the United Nations to Turkey, India, Greece, Pakistan, and Iran in the late 1960s and early 1970s. In 1982, he received the U.S. Public Service Award. Professor Linowes has served as a member of the board of directors of several major corporations.

He is the author of *Managing Growth Through Acquisition, Strategies for Survival, The Corporate Conscience,* and *The Impact of the Communication and Computer Revolution on Society* (Editor).